175 Y

o

St. Augustine's Parish Tunbridge Wells 1838-2013

A history

John Cunningham

May 2013

Published in Great Britain in May 2013 by
St. Augustine's Catholic Church,
Tunbridge Wells,
in association with
The Royal Tunbridge Wells Civic Society.
All rights reserved.

No part of this publication may be reproduced,
stored in a retrieval system, or transmitted,
in any form or by any means,
without the prior permission
of the copyright holder.

Within the UK, exceptions are allowed
in respect of any 'fair dealing' for the purpose of
research or private study, or criticism or review,
as permitted under
The Copyright, Design and Patents Act,1988.

© St. Augustine's Catholic Church, Tunbridge Wells, 2013

The author has asserted his right to be identified
as the author of this work in accordance
with the Copyright, Design and Patents Act, 1988

The Publishers have made every effort to establish the copyright
of all extracts and illustrations in this monograph
and apologise for any unwitting oversight or omission.

ISBN 978-0-9560944-4-5

The text is set in Bookman Old Style 10 pt.
and the cover in Bookman Old Style 12 – 30 pt

Front and back covers:
St Augustine's Church, Grosvenor Road, 1840
St. Augustine's Church, Crescent Road, 2013

Printed and bound by
TMS, Paddock Wood, Kent TN12 6DP

CONTENTS

Page

Contents

Foreword

Chapter

1.	The Historical and Religious Background	1
2.	The Progress from Mission to Parish	8
3.	The Locations and the Buildings	11
4.	The Priests of the Parish	31
5.	The Size of the Parish	50
6.	New Parishes and More Mass Centres	57
7.	The Congregation	65
8.	The Life of the Parish	80
9.	The Schools of the Parish	98
10.	Church Finances	112

The Future   120

Acknowledgments   122

Sources   122

Bibliography   122

Appendices

1.	Parish Priests and Assistant Priests	123
2.	Visiting Priests	126
3.	Parish Statistics	127
4.	Parish boundaries as 'canonically erected', 1970	128

Index   129

FOREWORD
by
Canon Peter Stodart,
Parish Priest of
St. Augustine's Catholic Church, Tunbridge Wells

This is not the first history of St. Augustine's Catholic Church in Tunbridge Wells.

A very comprehensive history, entitled "One Cog", was written by Ted Marchant, parishioner, convert and journalist, which covered its origins up to 1969 and his text was extended to 1995 by Chris Storr, another parishioner and parish organist, so that it could be published as a 232-page history in 1995. "One Cog", which often treated of wider Catholic and Diocesan issues than the Parish itself, was a broadly chronological and narrative history and is very detailed.

In celebrating the 175th Anniversary of the foundation of St. Augustine's, the organising committee agreed that there was a good case for updating the history of the church, but the temporal, financial, logistic and stylistic restraints in doing so, raised too many problems in the time available. So it was decided that a shorter history should be produced which would not be chronological, but would treat differing aspects/issues of the Parish in separate chapters. That is what this history is. However, its debt to 'One Cog' and its authors, for the wealth of original data which they collected, is indisputable and should be publicly acknowledged.

I would also like to acknowledge and thank John Cunningham, the Tunbridge Wells local historian and one of our parishioners, for sieving, researching and writing this history and his team of Parish Archivists, Gillian Shinar, Bridget Adam, Pat Cookson and Carla Davis, who spent so many hours trawling through our Archives.

We hope that the reader will be interested, informed, and pleased by what we are offering.

Canon Peter Stodart

Grosvenor Road, with St. Augustine's on the right, 25th September 1840. One of a series of some 60 prints of Tunbridge Wells, which Rock & Co. produced between 1840 and 1865.

CHAPTER 1 The Historical and Religious Background

When St. Augustine's Church was built in Tunbridge Wells in 1838, England was a strongly Protestant country with a record of 250-300 years of anti-Catholic feelings.

Until the mid-16th century, England had been a Catholic country as until then, the Catholic Church had been the only form of *established* Christian Church in Western Europe. The English Reformation started as a schism, a division in the *organisation and structure* of the Church, by Henry VIII when for his own dynastic and personal reasons, he took over the control and leadership of the Church in England from the Pope. It was turned fairly quickly by the intelligentsia and academics of the day into a division over *doctrine,* which made the English Reformation not only a schismatic, but also an heretical movement by the conventional theological standards of that time.

These divisions were aggravated by the Pope being then both an active temporal ruler[1] as well as the spiritual leader in Europe; and by England's two traditional enemies, France and Spain, remaining Catholic during the European Reformation.

In 16th and 17th century England, religion was probably the most important driving force/subject for discussion/influence in everyday life, just as politics and the economy hold a similar position in the 20th and 21st centuries. This is why the issue of religion, of Catholic v. Protestant, became the dominant *political* issue, coupled with the related issue of loyalty to the Crown and by an accompanying paranoia among the English about the likelihood of being invaded by foreigners, who were seen almost by definition as being Catholic.

Feelings did run high on both sides and some of each side were prepared to go to extreme measures to achieve what they believed and wanted. There were plots, none successful, which were suppressed with much cruelty and Catholics were 'branded' *Roman* Catholics in 1622 by King James I to emphasise their supposed

---

[1] Of the Papal States, in what we now know as central Italy, with 16,000 sq. miles and a population of 1-2 million in the 16th century.

[2] Emigration from Ireland, due to the Potato Famine (during which 25% of the

disloyalty to the Crown and their alleged allegiance to another foreign power; a deliberately pejorative description which lingers on in common parlance to this day, without most people appreciating its original derogatory meaning, or significance.

This antagonism continued throughout the 17th century and well into the 18th century; as late as 1780, the anti-Catholic Gordon Riots had the citizens of London 'quaking in their boots'. Even Tunbridge Wells, 35 miles from London, had troops stationed there, on call to quell any disturbance in the capital or region.

Tolerance of Catholicism was growing. There had been two Catholic Relief Acts in 1778 (which had contributed to the Gordon Riots) and 1791, which had removed a number of restrictions. The first suspended some of the Penal Laws, providing that you registered as 'a Papist' with your local magistrate and swore an Oath of Allegiance to George III. The second of 1791 allowed Catholic churches/chapels, which up till then did not [at least officially] exist, to be registered with a magistrate and so allowed Mass to be celebrated publicly in Great Britain for the first time since the 16th century. These led the way to the third Catholic Relief Act of 1829, more often referred to as the Catholic Emancipation Act, which granted full civil and political liberties to British Catholics (including all the Irish) for the first time.

It is in this context, just nine years after the Act, that St. Augustine's Church came to be built in Tunbridge Wells. At that time there were understandably very few Catholic churches in England since all the medieval Catholic churches had been turned into Anglican churches at the Reformation; and St. Augustine's must have been one of the first Catholic churches to have been built in England since the Middle Ages.

Up till then, the minority who still clung after three centuries to their Catholic Faith, were likely to be either the aristocracy who were *relatively* 'above the law', or inhabitants of the more distant parts of the country (such as Cheshire and Lancashire) which were in practical terms beyond the control of the Recusancy Laws, but neither had churches which they could attend and Mass had to be heard in private houses. However there was a large increase in the number of Catholics in England following the Irish Potato Famine of 1846-48[2] and this increased the need for churches to be built.

But there is no record of much Catholic activity in Tunbridge Wells, as such, until the early 19th century. There were places in the neighbourhood where a zealous Catholic might find Mass. The leading one was Scotney Castle at Lamberhurst which remained in the hands of the Catholic Darrell family until 1774. There were also the Whyborne family in Pembury until 1660 and from 1600-1740, the Whetenhall family in East Peckham. From about 1813, Mass could be heard in Tunbridge Wells *in the summer season* at Jerningham House on Mount Sion, celebrated by the Jerningham family chaplain. There is also a record in the Archives of the Diocese of Southwark of the Harting family having a house with a private chapel on Bishop's Down, which they visited every summer from 1813-38, bringing their own Catholic chaplain with them.

The Catholics of the area did not have a church to which they could go, while all the other Protestant denominations in Tunbridge Wells already had at least one. The first Protestant church was Anglican and was 'a Chappel', the Chapel of King Charles the Martyr but not called so in print until 1733. It was first built in 1678, just 72 years after the discovery of the Wells, enlarged in 1682 and doubled in size in the 1690s. It was however still a 'chapel-of-ease' since Tunbridge Wells was then part of the parish of Tunbridge (now called Tonbridge) and remained so until 1889[3].

The Low Church/Non-Conformist presence and influence in Tunbridge Wells had been there since early times, despite the location's distinct Royalist and Court associations, witness the somewhat Biblical location names of Mount Sion, Mount Ephraim and Mount Pleasant. Presbyterians first met at Mount Ephraim House from 1689 and then subsequently in 1720 built an Independent Chapel for Presbyterians. The Emmanuel Chapel, initially a wooden chapel belonging to the Countess of Huntingdon's Connexion (an 'upper class' offshoot of the Methodists) was next

---

[2] Emigration from Ireland, due to the Potato Famine (during which 25% of the population of Ireland are estimated to have died), reached its peak in 1847, with an oft-quoted figure for that year alone of 300.000 Irish emigrants, about half of whom stayed in Great Britain, the rest going to the USA, Australia and elsewhere.
[3] Interestingly, the historic layout of the Chapel confirms its inherent Low Church style, since a Chancel, a Sanctuary and an Altar were only introduced in 1882.

and opened on Mount Ephraim in 1769. Over the next 98 years it was transformed into a fine Gothic-style Church, with a spire 140 ft. high, which dominated the Tunbridge Wells skyline, until it was demolished in 1974 to provide better car park access for the now-superceded Kent & Sussex Hospital.

A year after the foundation of the Emmanuel Chapel, a Baptist Chapel was opened next to Mount Ephraim House. In 1830, the Congregationalists opened first in a Chapel on Mount Sion, moving in 1848 because they needed more room to Mount Pleasant, opposite the site of what became the Opera House in 1902. It is a reflection of the times that subsequently this elegant, porticoed Congregational Church became a Habitat shop; and the Opera House a pub.

In 1833, the Particular (or Calvinist) Baptists built themselves a chapel in Hanover Road which is still there, to which St. Augustine's would become adjacent in 1838.

This highly-moral Low Church/Non-Conformist presence in Tunbridge Wells in the late 18th/early 19th. century was in marked contrast to what had been the behaviour of visitors to ' the town' in the 17th and 18th centuries, when they were noted for their often-more-than-risqué behaviour.

'King Charles the Martyr' remained the only Anglican church in Tunbridge Wells until 1827, when the development, by John Ward and his architect Decimus Burton, of what was initially called Calverley New Town included the building of a completely new Church, Holy Trinity, with a capacity of 1,500 to cope with the expected congregation from the new development. It would quickly be followed in 1835 by Christ Church in the High Street.

So the reader will appreciate that by the time St. Augustine's was opened in 1838, there were already three Anglican churches and five Non-Conformist chapels in Tunbridge Wells, for what was estimated in 1831 to be a population of 5,929, but which was shown in the Census of 1841 to have grown to 8,302, an increase of 40% in just ten years.

All these churches, whether Anglican or Non-Conformist, were Low Church in their theology and liturgy and more anti-Catholic than was usual among the increasingly tolerant Anglican Church, which was changing under the influence of the Oxford Movement[4]. However Holy Trinity would, if anything, become more Low Church under the influence of the Rev. (later Canon) Edward Hoare, who came to Tunbridge Wells in 1853; and stayed until his death in 1893. The Hoare family were Quakers and City Bankers and Edward's aunt was the Quaker prison reformer, Elisabeth Fry. He and his parents were received into the Anglican Church and it is somewhat surprising, in view of the Quaker tradition of tolerance, that the Rev. Hoare was so aggressively adverse to any religious beliefs other than his own. As Canon Hoare, he was to become the major influence on the moral and religious life of Tunbridge Wells in the late 19th century.

With the coming of the railway in 1846, the population of Tunbridge Wells expanded considerably to 13,807 in 1861 and 24,309 in 1881 and this led to Canon Hoare opening 'daughter' parishes: St. John's in 1858; St. James's in 1860; and St. Peter's 1874. He ran into problems however with the building of the Mission Chapel of St. Stephen for the poorer northerly area of the town in 1870, which would be superceded by the Parish of St. Barnabas in 1881, when the incumbent of both of these chose to be High, rather than Low Anglican. Nonetheless Canon Hoare's influence was still dominant in the town and St. Augustine's must almost certainly have had problems with him.

In this context, it should be explained that in 1838, Catholicism in England and Wales had no proper organisational structure. There was no diocesan hierarchy, no dioceses, no parishes as such. The Catholic Church in England and Wales had had 22 dioceses immediately before the Reformation, but all of these had been taken over by the new Anglican Church. From 1623, Catholicism was governed in England and Wales by an Apostolic Vicar, appointed by and acting for the Pope. At first, there was only one Apostolic Vicar, then it was increased to four, each with a separate district – London, Midland, Northern and Western – and each district was divided into a number of 'Missions' which were very much larger than parishes. In 1840, the number of Apostolic Vicars was doubled to eight and finally, the full Catholic hierarchy was re-established

---

[4] A group of Anglicans, of whom John Henry Newman was a prominent member, who in the 1830s attempted to reform the Church of England by restoring high-church traditions. While Newman became a Catholic (and later a Cardinal), many of the group developed into what was called Anglo-Catholicism.

by the Papal Bull *Universalis Ecclesiae* in 1850. It created 12 Catholic dioceses without seeking any 'permission' to do so from any established 'authority' in England, an event which caused great disquiet among many Anglicans, including Queen Victoria herself. 'Am I Queen of England, or not?', she asked.

So when St. Augustine's was built in 1838, it was not a parish because no Diocesan structure existed, but a Mission centre for a very much wider area which stretched from Riverhead near Sevenoaks in the north, to Rye on the South Coast; and from Edenbridge on the west, to Cranbrook in the east; and so it included the towns of Sevenoaks, Tonbridge, Crowborough and Uckfield. A major part of its history has been how this Mission turned into a Parish and how this Parish shrank in size, as it spawned new Parishes which in due course became independent of it.

The obvious question to be asked is why the Jesuits chose Tunbridge Wells as the *centre* for their new Mission, when until recently it had been little more than a village, and a seasonal 'tourist' village at that. There is no definitive answer to this question, but it is probable that Tunbridge Wells was considered to be a more *central* location for the Mission than other towns in the area. The Mission boundaries would in part have been dictated by the existing boundaries of neighbouring Missions; in terms of ease of communication and travel in the days before railways, the historic road (now the A21) which has run through the centre of the area from north to south for over a thousand years, may also have been a factor. It should be noted that the Railway, although a great topic of discussion, was not to come to the area for another 10-15 years.

Finally, in terms of the historical context of the period, the reader should remember that the mid-19th century was a time of great change and upheaval in both Britain and Europe. The parishioners of St. Augustine's, although maybe not as well informed as we are today, would have been aware, and in many respects fearful, about the course of events in both.

In Europe, there were revolutions in France in July 1830 and February 1848; Garibaldi and Mazzini with the Risorgimento movement from about 1848 were 'liberating' and uniting Italy, including the Papal States which finally ceased to exist in 1870; and the fragmented former states of the Holy Roman Empire were being coalesced, first by the German Confederation created in 1815, then the Zollverein (Customs Union) in the 1830-40s and finally from 1860, by Bismarck into the new German Empire; and by the Emperor Franz Joseph I of Austria in south-eastern Europe, although he already 'owned' most of it in terms of practical control, into the Austro-Hungarian Empire.

While Britain was externally at peace for nearly 40 years, from 1815 until the Crimean War in 1854, internally it was adjusting in socio-economic terms to the impact of the Industrial Revolution (the Peterloo Massacre of 1819, the Luddite movement, the Tolpuddle Martyrs); and in religious terms to the Evangelical Revival[5] and with the somewhat conflicting aims of the Oxford Movement which came later. All these caused potential strife, which occasionally verged almost on revolution.

---

[5] The Evangelical Movement or Revival began within the Church of England in the 18th century and preceded the Oxford Movement. John Wesley, the founder of Methodism, was one of its major inspirations, and he and his followers eventually left the Church of England, but many with very similar beliefs remained within the established Church. This Evangelical wing, particularly William Wilberforce and the Clapham sect, were inspired to combat social ills at home and slavery abroad, and founded Bible and missionary societies. It is often maintained that Evangelical Revivalism directed working-class attention during the Industrial Revolution toward moral regeneration, and not social radicalism: and therefore England avoided most of the socio-economic tensions which had caused the French Revolution.

CHAPTER 2 THE PROGRESS FROM MISSION TO PARISH

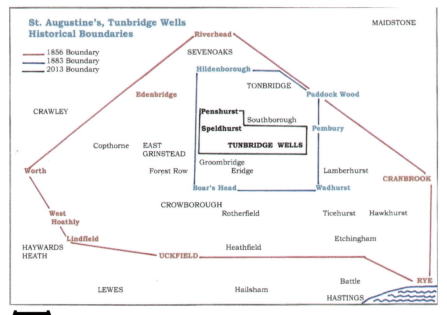

The boundary (red line above) for the Mission which was established in Tunbridge Wells in 1838 stretched from:

Riverhead (north of Sevenoaks) to Cranbrook and Rye on the South Coast; and from Edenbridge on the west to Worth, Uckfield and Rye in the east; and so it included the towns of

Sevenoaks, Tonbridge, Cranbrook, Crowborough and Uckfield.

During the Jesuit Mission period (1838-1867), two independent Parishes were also established on the borders of this area, but outside:
Chislehurst: St. Mary   (1852; 1854; consecrated 1943)[6]
Lewes: St. Pancras   (1865, 1870, 1939; consecrated 1962)

---

[6] Dates: the first is the foundation date of the Parish; the second (or the third if there is one) is the date of the *current* church.
Consecration was only allowed when a Church was free of any debt.

Following the transfer of the Mission to the Diocese in 1867 and up to 1883, when the boundary of the Mission area was reduced, a further five separate and independent parishes were founded in the area:

East Grinstead: Our Lady & St. Peter (1879; 1898; consecrated 1899)
Heron's Ghyll, Uckfield: St. John the Evangelist (1879; 1897; consecrated 1904)
Sevenoaks: St. Thomas of Canterbury (1880; 1896; consecrated 1935)
Goudhurst: Sacred Heart (1882)
Uckfield: Our Lady Immaculate & St. Philip Neri (1885; 1945; 1958; consecrated 1961)

In 1883 the boundary of what was still a Mission was shrunk to within a line (blue line above) which ran from Hildenborough (north of Tonbridge) to Boar's Head (just north of Crowborough) and to Eridge, then over to Wadhurst and north to Pembury and back to Hildenborough, an area which would be difficult to cover today, even with a car. The new boundary still left the Rector of Tunbridge Wells with a large area to cover, which included four locations which would become separate and independent parishes in due course, namely:

Tonbridge: Corpus Christi (1894; 1904; consecrated 1985)
Paddock Wood: St. Justus (1949; 1950; new church 1981; consecrated 1981)
Pembury:St.Anselm's: (1965)
Southborough: St. Dunstan's (1950; 1969; consecrated 1984)

Five other locations which were in the original Mission area did not become parishes until after 1883:

Diocese of Southwark
Cranbrook: St. Theodore (1937; 1958: consecrated 1991)
Edenbridge: St. Lawrence (1931; 1952; consecrated 1981)

Diocese of Arundel & Brighton
(*a new Diocese formed in 1965 out of the Diocese of Southwark*)
Crowborough: St. Mary, Mother of Christ: (1910; 1923; 1936)
Rye: St. Anthony of Padua (1900; 1930; consecrated 1933)
Wadhurst:Sacred Heart (1929)

St. Augustine's did not technically become a Parish until April 1901 when it was raised to the status of a parish.[7] Since 1887 the specific definition of the Parish boundaries has been amended slightly to accommodate minor adjustments, such as Wadhurst in 1929 and Groombridge in 1970; and the latest definition (1970) of its boundaries 'canonically erected' will be found in Appendix 4.

Today the Parish boundaries are broadly those of the old Borough of Royal Tunbridge Wells, which was created in 1889 and lasted until the national re-organisation of local government in 1974, which created the new extended Borough of Tunbridge Wells. There is however one minor variation in the Parish's boundaries compared with the Borough: Penshurst which in local government terms is in Sevenoaks, is within St. Augustine's Parish.

✧✧✧✧✧

(Note: While the Church in Tunbridge Wells was dedicated to St. Augustine from the beginning, it was not generally referred to as such when it first opened, being generally called just 'the Catholic Chapel', even by Catholics.)

---

[7]Terminology can be confusing, particularly when it is used loosely. Today the terms Rector and Parish Priest are often used almost interchangeably, but there is both a technical and a canonical difference. Technically a Mission is an embryonic quasi-Parish and the Priest in charge is normally called a Rector, who can be changed/removed by his superior without any need of explanation. A Parish is canonically an established designated area where the priest-in-charge is titled Parish Priest and has total authority and cannot be removed, except for misconduct. In English-speaking countries, many so-called parishes are however not canonical parishes.

CHAPTER 3   THE LOCATIONS AND THE BUILDINGS

St. Augustine's has occupied two sites in its 175-year history.

The first was at the junction of Grosvenor Road and Hanover Road, where it was for 129 years from 1838 to 1967, when the site was sold as the Church building was considered to be both far too small for its growing congregation, and also incapable of expansion within Planning Regulations.

It was also incurably damp and the cost of necessary refurbishment of the old building was considered uneconomic.

Part of Britton's Map of Tunbridge Wells, 1832

The second is at Crescent Road, between Calverley Park and what is now the Hotel du Vin (formerly the Calverley Hotel and previously Calverley House), where it has been from 1975 to the present day.

In between 1967 and 1975, St. Augustine's was somewhat peripatetic, Mass being said variously at the Sacred Heart Convent in Pembury Road; St. Gregory's School in Reynold's Lane; at Greystones, a house in Crescent Road belonging to two parishioners, Dr. Ken Ross and his wife, Dr. Mary Ross, before it was demolished for the new St. Augustine's to be built there; and finally at what was familiarly and somewhat irreverently known as St. Tesco's, which was the hall above the Tesco's supermarket which was built in 1971 on the site of the original St. Augustine's Church.

HANOVER ROAD

The choice of the Hanover Road site by the Jesuits, which would have been undeveloped open land at that time, was indirectly due to John Ward who, with Decimus Burton as his architect, decided in 1826 to develop some 56 acres of the 874 acres he owned to the north of the 'village' of Tunbridge Wells as 'Calverley New Town'. This development was intended to be separate from Tunbridge Wells, which was only about a mile away, but its proximity and the established awareness and reputation of Tunbridge Wells meant that the new name never caught on and the development was slowly absorbed into the existing Tunbridge Wells. It has redounded to the reputation of both Decimus Burton and Tunbridge Wells ever since.

It is a reasonable surmise that anyone intending to build in Tunbridge Wells at that time would look most probably to the north of the town, to the so-called Calverley New Town, as the best area to do so. The land the Jesuits acquired was outside the Ward estate and from the Conveyance dated 22nd/23rd March, 1837, it would seem that it had been bought by Henry Hopkins from George Camfield in 1835, sold by Henry Hopkins to John Thomas in 1836, and sold by John Thomas to the Jesuits in 1837. The price the Jesuits paid was £756.16s.7d.

The site at Hanover Road would around 1900 have a frontage of 118 ft on to Grosvenor Road and 136 ft on to Hanover Road, making it just over a third of an acre (0.37, to be precise). But initially the Grosvenor Road frontage was longer and the Hanover Road shorter. There is evidence in the Jesuit Archives at Farm Street that some land with a frontage onto Grosvenor Road was sold in November 1860 to Mr. Benedetto Bianchi for £306, which was about 40% of the price of all the land bought 23 years earlier in 1837. It therefore seems probable that Mr. Bianchi in buying the land, also developed it as a row of shops. The Grosvenor Road frontage of 118 ft never changed after 1860, but the Hanover Road frontage increased in

1888 to 136 ft when Brunswick Villa next door to the Church in Hanover Road was bought; its subsequent demolition in the early 20th century would eventually enable the School to be expanded.

The original church was designed in Palladian style by Joseph Ireland (1780-1841) a well-known architect of the day and built of the local sandstone which was a feature of Calverley New Town. It had a length of 70 ft fronting on to Grosvenor Road and a width of 34 ft fronting on to Hanover Road. The total cost for the land and the building was £5,400.2s.0d., of which the land cost was £756.16s.7d. and most of the cost (£3,921 or 73%) was funded by the Jesuits. It was also paid for in part 'by subscription' which has always been taken up till now to mean 'by wealthy Catholic donors', but evidence recently brought to light suggests that the Jesuits may have sought donation from the non-Catholic shopkeepers of Tunbridge Wells as well[8]. However the Jesuit accounts do not reflect this, since they show the public subscriptions were received mainly through two companies, Wright & Co. of London, and Beeching & Co. of Tunbridge.

To the south of the Church, the frontage on to Grosvenor Road was occupied by a house which was the Presbytery and which was built just before the Church. To the west was a small open space which to the south was the garden of the Presbytery, and above it fronting onto Hanover Road, was undeveloped land which would in due course provide space for the Church Campanile and the original School. The acquisition of Brunswick Villa would allow for further

---

[8] The Rev. John Cumming, a Scottish Low Church minister with a house on Tunbridge Wells Common, reported at the Protestant Reformation Society Annual Meeting in London in May 1839 that " at Tunbridge Wells a person came to arrange about the erection of a (Roman Catholic) chapel; he got men and women singers in order to set forth the beauty, attractions and splendour of this idolatrous system. He went to several shop-keepers at Tunbridge Wells and told them, that if they would contribute towards the chapel, so many more of the higher classes would be visitors, there would be twice as many customers at their shops and inns, and they would thereby realise twice the income. It will, added the papal advocate, be the best speculation you ever engaged in if you only contribute to the chapel at Tunbridge Wells. Some were weak and base enough to sell their birthright for a mess of pottage. (cheers)".

Part of the report above may be true, although there is no secondary evidence for it, but claiming that male and female singers 'serenaded' the shopkeepers seems a little over the top, even by the standards of anti-Catholicism in Tunbridge Wells in the 19th century.

expansion of the School in the future. The blueprint plan below prepared for insurance purposes in 1923 shows clearly how the site was developed with the single-storey Old School built in 1877 (C) and the single-storey New School built in 1907 (C).

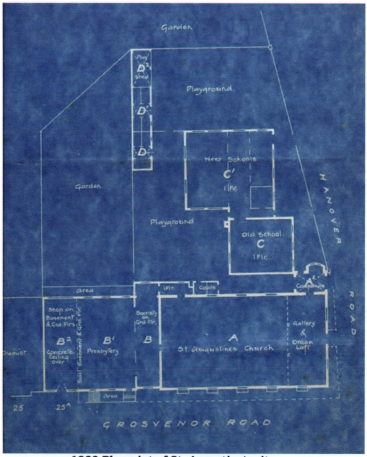

1923 Blueprint of St. Augustine's site

Little happened on the site until the Jesuit Mission in Tunbridge Wells came to a close in 1866. It then took some time for Fr. Joseph Searle, the new Diocesan priest who would be St. Augustine's first Rector and serve for the next 33 years until his death in 1899, to assess what he had been given.

The two events in his pastoral mission which had a major impact on the Parish and the Town, were the foundation of St. Augustine's School and the Campanile. St. Augustine's School no longer occupies its original site and has gone through many developments, but it still thrives today on different sites as St. Augustine's Primary School and St. Gregory's Comprehensive School. However the Campanile is no more: the Clock survived until 1967, but its Carillon ceased its ringing during the First World War.

The 1870 Education Act laid down that all children (male or *female*) aged 5–12 must attend a primary school. On 17th July, 1870 in the Church notices, parents are warned that they must send their children to school. On 25th September 1870, parents are reminded again and on 8th July 1871, there was yet another reminder.

It is not clear from the Archives when exactly St. Augustine's became involved in providing a school for its children. There is a reference in Fr. Searle's 'round-robin' letter and appeal of 5th March, 1867 of the need to support the Poor Schools and maintain the 'fabrics of the Church, Presbytery *and School'*. So a School building existed in 1867. There is also an unverified note in the Archives for 1938 which says that it was built in 1852, and there are also Planning applications to the Tunbridge Wells Board in the 1870s for a new School building and alterations, but there is no evidence about what preceded it.

In 1887, the year of Queen Victoria's Golden Jubilee, and as part of St. Augustine's celebrations, the crypt was 'improved' to be lit by gas, whose jets had domes to extract the fumes (the very latest development of the times) and turned into a schoolroom with a capacity for 270 pupils (an astonishing and somewhat unbelievable figure), for what were said to be 'an increasing number of pupils'. This is somewhat puzzling but more of this in the Chapters on the Schools. This improvement cost £374.15s.3d and was paid for by Mrs. Fenwick, a widow and a convert, in memory of her son, Walter, also a convert, who had died that year. Mrs. Fenwick lived nearby at 'Cintra', 32 Upper Grosvenor Road.

But there were two other major events for St. Augustine's for the Jubilee Year which was almost the 50th Anniversary of the foundation of the Church. First, the installation of a multi-coloured marble altar and second, the laying by the Countess de Bayona of the Foundation Stone for the Campanile, or bell-tower, which would not be complete until 1888. (See Chapter 7 for more details about the Count de Bayona).

Count De Bayona,

later to be the Marquis de Misa

Church, Campanile and School

The event which long-term had the greatest impact on the lives of the inhabitants of Tunbridge Wells was without doubt the Campanile. The Campanile was paid for by the Count and Countess de Bayona, who lived in Tunbridge Wells and were parishioners. It was rectangular in shape, being 10ft. wide on its front elevation and 15 ft. wide on its side elevation, with a height of 68 ft and it filled a small gap between the Church and the School House built in 1877. The architect was Brett F. Elphick, of 7 Great Queen St., Westminster and the builder John Jarvis, a well-established business in Tunbridge Wells which only closed down in 2009.

The Campanile had a Turret Clock with two 4-ft faces and five bells weighing a ton. The bells could be rung i.e. swung, or chimed i.e. hit with a hammer. Each bell therefore had a clapper for ringing and a hammer for chiming. The hour bell was struck only once an hour but the other four chimed in a sequence referred to as the Westminster Quarters, using a special mechanism called an Ellacombe Chiming apparatus. The ringing of the bells of course required a team of five men and it was difficult to get enough men to do it because it was hard work, but generally they were rung on Sundays for 20 minutes before the 11 am Mass and the 6.30 pm Evening Service, with just a single bell ringing for the five minutes before the start of the service. The names of these stalwarts should be recorded for posterity - Mr. Edwards who was the first to ring them, Tom & Alfred Hubble, William & Laurie Vinehill, Jack Chapman, Charles Marsh and Joseph Walton. They had a number of 'changes' to ring, including a special one for weddings. The clock was made and the bells cast by Messrs. Gillett at their Steam Clock Factory in Croydon and cost £295.11s.11d.

The Clock overlooked both Grosvenor and Hanover Roads and could be seen *and heard* from hundreds of yards. There can be no question that the clock and bells must have made the inhabitants very aware of the presence of the Catholic Church in Tunbridge Wells. The quarterly chimes throughout the night must have been particularly irritating. In 1901, the recently-in-charge Fr. Stapley did ask the manufacturers if something could be done about this. Their reply was that it was possible and at a cost of only £7.10s.0d, but it was not recommended as 'it will make a complication of the mechanism (which) is very unusual'.

The plans for the Campanile, as published in 'The Builder' of 15th June 1888.
Note that it says that the Upper (Bell) Chamber will have a chime of 18 bells – in the end, there were only five.

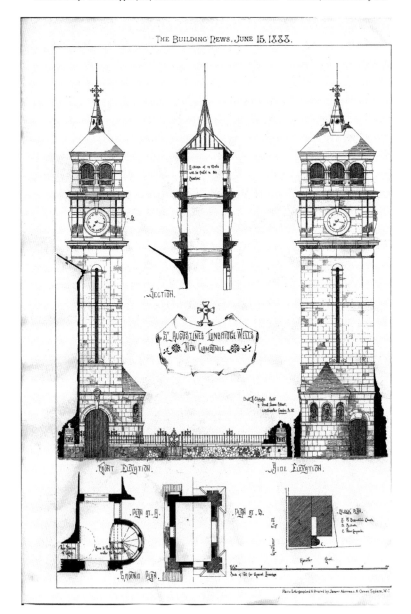

The clock played a part in the lives of all those who lived and worked within earshot, because it was designated an official timekeeper under the Factories Act and it continued to chime for 88 years. Alfred Hubble used to say that for many years a common remark among workmen was "I don't care what your watch says. Mine's right by the Catholic."

The Westminster Chimes had a shorter life of only about 27 years, because they were silenced in 1915 when the staff at the General Hospital, which was on the opposite side of Grosvenor Road, complained that they were disturbing the wounded soldiers who were patients at the Hospital. Possibly because it was said that the brickwork of the tower had weakened, or possibly because it was not popular with the 'neighbours', or a combination of these reasons, but the Chimes were never rung again, except on 11th. November 1918 by Alfred Hubble to mark the end of 'the war to end all wars'.

The Presbytery was next door to the Church, with shops next door to it. In the beginning, there was a gap the width of a shop between the Presbytery and the shops, but in 1900 this space was infilled by Fr. Stapley to provide another separate shop on the ground floor, with the two upper floors being attached to the Presbytery and providing more bedrooms.

An inventory, taken in 1930 for the purpose of insurance (which incidentally valued its contents at £913.13s-0d)[9] gives details of the Presbytery which show that it was on four floors – Basement, Ground, First and Second Floors, with an extension of three rooms on two floors over the next door shop. The Basement was the kitchen, larder, scullery and cellar. The Ground Floor was the Hall, Dining Room and Mission Room; the First Floor three bedrooms, with a fourth one over the shop, and the Rector's Room, the Curates' Sitting Room, a bathroom and a WC; and the Second Floor was a fifth bedroom called the Bishop's Room, but presumably for visitors, and a lumber room, with two further rooms referred to as the Maids' Wing over the next door shop.

---

[9] A subsequent Inventory prepared in 1943 for the same purpose valued the contents at £2,026-10s-9d, with the Library valued at £437-6s-0d, not just books but fittings.

Britain was very quick to honour its War dead – the Cenotaph in Whitehall was dedicated just a year later on 11th November, 1919 and almost every town and village followed suit in the next three years.

St. Augustine's, possibly because it was a parish, rather than a town or a village where all sorts of people had to be consulted, was probably among the very first to do so, since its memorial was dedicated just one month after the end of the War on 11th December 1918.

It had actually been planned since 7th July 1918 when Canon Keatinge announced that it had been proposed to erect a memorial on the Grosvenor Road wall of the church and donations were invited. There was a very quick response and the fund was soon oversubscribed, and the memorial, which was to be a huge wooden crucifix, was commissioned from Messrs. Wall of Cheltenham. It was delivered on 17th November and aroused great interest among Catholics and also the anti-Catholic element in the town, who declared in somewhat unrighteous indignation that 'It will frighten the horses'.

The unveiling and dedication was announced for 11th December at 3.30pm. Threats were made to set the Memorial on fire and so several members of the Guild of the Blessed Sacrament stood guard over it the previous night. Canon Keatinge also astutely invited the Mayor, Mr. (later Sir) Robert Gower, whose wife was a Catholic, to unveil the Memorial, knowing that the Mayor's presence would automatically trigger a police presence at the ceremony. The Mayor made an appropriate speech and the Canon's brother, Bishop William Keatinge, who was a Chaplain-General (equivalent to the rank of Brigadier-General) in the Army, consecrated it 'in memory of our brave fellow townsmen who made the supreme sacrifice'.

The Memorial listed 25 members of the Parish and its Crucifix now hangs in the narthex of the new St. Augustine's in Crescent Road.

The Unveiling of the War Memorial in December 1918

The War Memorial in 1920

The General Hospital in Grosvenor Road, opposite St. Augustine's Church

St. Augustine's illuminated for the Coronation, 1937

The view of the Church from the Chancel, which never changed.

The Chancel in the 1890s, with gas lighting standards

The Chancel in the 1920s   The Chancel in 1967 before demolition
with electricity and other changes.

St. Augustine's in Hanover Road was never an entirely satisfactory building. It had been built to seat 250 people at a time when there probably at best 50 Catholics in Tunbridge Wells, but the congregation soon grew to exceed capacity (at least in theory). By 1898, there were 488 Catholics in the parish (a wider parish than today), of whom 313 were recorded as definitely 'practising'. So, over time, the parish learned to hold more than one Mass on Sundays, but over time the overcrowding would still get worse.

The building also suffered from damp. Tunbridge Wells is riddled with streams, most of them underground and unknown even to this day, and it is highly probable that one flows in the vicinity of the Church. Certainly the contractors building the new Tesco supermarket found that they had problems with water in the foundations. There were also increasing problems with noise with the arrival of the motor car and the general increase in traffic in Grosvenor Road, even on a Sunday morning before Sunday trading was introduced. The building was getting older and was probably not very well-built in the beginning, so the cost of renovation and repair was daunting.

Last Mass 23rd October 1967 by Archbishop Cowderoy, with (L to R) Frs. Michael Bunce, William Howell, Bernard Hegarty and Geoffrey Nixon

It is not surprising that over time the feeling grew in the Parish that a new Church was needed. On the site? Elsewhere? Could the land occupied by the old School (closed since 1963) be used? Would a T- or L-shaped church be possible, incorporating the old Church? These ideas proved impractical because of Planning Regulations which demanded space on site for car parking – in those days, one space for every 10 worshippers – so it was not possible. The Diocese of Southwark, who were its residual owners, decided to sell the site and it went for £80,000 to Tesco Supermarkets. The Last Mass at St. Augustine's in Hanover Road was celebrated by Dr. Cyril Cowderoy, the Archbishop of Southwark, on 23rd October, 1967.

The money was to be put aside to fund the new Church, although some suggested, somewhat euphorically in those ultra-idealistic post-Vatican II days, that it should be given instead to the African Missions.

But the big question was where should the new Church be?

Two centrally-located Anglican churches – Holy Trinity and Christchurch – which were potentially on offer, were considered early on, but were rejected. The new chapel built in 1963 at Beechwood Sacred Heart Convent was also offered for a similar sum, but this was rejected as being not sufficiently central and too isolated. This did not however stop the chapel being used as an interim 'stop-gap' venue for Sunday Mass, until a more central location could be found. For similar reasons, the Chapel at St. Gregory's School was also used for Sunday Mass, but both these were interim solutions, being used from the end of 1967 until 1971, when the Hall above Tesco's became ready for use.

Sacred Heart Convent Chapel, built in 1963

Part of the sale agreement with Tesco's had been that St. Augustine's would take a 99-year lease on the Hall above the supermarket to use it as a Parish Hall, at a cost of £38,000. While the Hall was not considered suitable as a Church on a long-term basis, it was acceptable short-term because it was more central than St. Gregory's or Beechwood Sacred Heart. So once Tesco's had built their supermarket, the Hall became the church from 1971 until the St. Augustine's of today was opened.

St. Augustine's Hall as a Chapel   St. Augustine's Hall, above Tesco's

CRESCENT ROAD

The site of St. Augustine's today had been a candidate since the very beginning, but there were problems which could have proved insuperable. It was then called 'Greystones' and was in Crescent Road. It was a large three-storey house, with an attachment called 'The Cottage' and with extensive grounds of nearly an acre, which lay between Calverley Park and what was then Cundall's Garage (but now is residential housing) and what is now the Hotel du Vin (but was formerly the Calverley Hotel and prior to that, Calverley House).

'Greystones' from the rear garden

It had been owned by the Countess Tankerville (1830-1921), widow of the 6th Earl, who was 20 years her senior; and she had lived there probably since the death of her husband in 1899. She died there in 1921 and the house was bought by a Catholic family, Dr. William Long, a pioneering radiologist, and his French wife and then occupied by their daughter, Dr. Mary Long and her husband Dr. Ken Ross, a New Zealander, who would emigrate to Durban, South Africa in October 1967.

Dr. Mary Ross and her father

For a long time Dr. Mary Ross had wanted St Augustine's to have the house, so that a new church and priests' house could be built on the site. The big issue was whether this would be allowed under Planning Regulations, or more precisely whether Tunbridge Wells Borough Council (TWBC) would give permission, or even more precisely whether the Councillors themselves would agree because somewhat surprisingly there were still some who in those days, just under 50 years ago, were known to be positively anti-Catholic.

The result was that it took some six years to obtain the necessary permission, but only a further two to build. Every possible objection was thrown at it:
- although hidden by trees, it would spoil the appearance of the 'historic' Calverley Grounds (and implicitly the view from Calverley Park), an opinion also shared by the Victorian Society in London;
- on the assumption that as a church, it would have some sort of tower or spire, this would spoil the skyline of Tunbridge Wells (this at a time when the 140–ft spire of Emmanuel Church still existed on Mount Ephraim; and TWBC had already approved the eight-storey office block in Forest Road, Hawkenbury, which used to dominate the town [but which thankfully was demolished in 2000]);
- it would increase the traffic in Crescent Road, particularly on Sundays, and disturb the neighbours (this at a time when they were just about to build a five-storey, 1000-capacity car park in Crescent Road directly opposite the proposed site);
- it was an unacceptable change-of-use from residential housing to church premises;
- the proposed 40 car-parking spaces would not be adequate - - true, but essentially only so on Sundays and Holidays-of-Obligation, and there would be a large car park opposite [which used to be free on Sundays, but is no longer].

While all this was going on, 'Greystones' had been bought from the Ross family for £35,000. It was initially used as a presbytery and parish office, with two rooms which opened up to make a very small chapel for use on a weekday, which could take up to 50 people, but which was not large enough for Sundays. So first the Sacred Heart Convent Chapel and St. Gregory's Chapel and then later the Hall above Tesco's, were used for Sunday services, with the Sacred Heart Chapel being retained for weddings and funerals, until a new Church was built.

No less than 7 planning applications were submitted and 6 rejected. The plan which was eventually approved by Tunbridge Wells Borough Council was by the architects, Robert Maguire & Keith Murray, and the church was built by Elkingtons of Tonbridge, a firm owned by Jack Elkington who lived in Southborough and built St. Dunstan's at the same time. The plan involved demolition of the main part of the house, leaving a two-storey section, called 'the Cottage', which would be converted in 2000 into a new Parish Hall (but even this took almost two years to get permission, yet only one year to build).

The Church was completed in the autumn of 1975 and was solemnly blessed by Archbishop Cyril Cowderoy. The cost had escalated from an estimate of £176,606 at tender in August 1974 to a final figure of £184,036 on completion. Some 125 parishioners made covenants which brought in just under £6,000 a year or £41,000 over the seven year period, and this together with the money already to hand, left the parish with a debt of approximately £65,000.

Taking into account the objections made, the plan imaginatively:
- kept most of the tall mature trees already on the site;
- replaced the three-storey house with a single-storey open-plan square church, with seating on three sides of the altar and with a pyramid roof with glazed ends, which made it less than two-storey;
- built the development into the side of the hill, so that the church was on the top level and the presbytery and other offices were somewhat unusually below the church.
-

In the circumstances, it is probably not surprising that this church is described in the Pevsner Architectural Guide to Kent as 'self-effacing'.

By Canon Law, a church cannot be consecrated until it is clear of all debt, so it is remarkable that the new St. Augustine's was able to be consecrated by the Most Rev. Michael Bowen, Archbishop of Southwark, on Saturday 24th May, 1980, less than five years after it was built.

The use of the Hall above Tesco's was retained, although latterly shared with Tunbridge Wells Christian Fellowship, until the new

Hall and meeting room complex at Crescent Road was completed in 2001. When the proposal was made in 1997 to build the new complex, a referendum was taken and 93% of the Parish voted in favour, but the building of this complex was fraught with opposition from elsewhere. Between January 1998 and April 1999, no less than four planning applications were made to and rejected by Tunbridge Wells Borough Council. An appeal was lodged against the last objection and a Planning Inspector adjudicated and found in favour of St. Augustine's. The estimated cost in 1997 was £190,000 but the contract sum agreed in February 2000 was £214,261. The final cost on completion was to reach £250,000. Fortunately, this was more than covered by the sale of a parish property at 28 Claremont Road.

St. Augustine's, Crescent Rd.

Church Hall, from rear   **Main Church Hall**

CHAPTER 4   THE PRIESTS OF THE PARISH

St. Augustine's has been blessed over its 175 years with the devotion of over 80 priests – some 7 Jesuit Missioners in the first 28 years from 1838-1866; 10 Diocesan Priests as Parish Priests (Rectors), plus 5 as Vicarius Adjutor, in the 147 years from 1866-2013; and no less than 65 Assistant Priests (formerly known as curates, until this title was changed by Vatican II) over a 119-year period from 1894. A full list of the priests of the parish with dates where recorded or known, will be found in Appendix 1. In addition, the Parish has benefitted from the presence of a large number of visiting priests, often for a matter of a few weeks and months, with many of them from abroad (Appendix 2); and also in the last 30 years from having at least one Deacon in the Parish.

THE JESUIT MISSIONERS
St. Augustine's opened its doors on 28th. May 1838, although it was not officially opened until Bishop Thomas Griffiths, the then Vicar Apostolic of the London Region, celebrated High Mass in the new church on 17th July 1838.

The nature of the Missioners' work was that while based in one place, they roamed around their Mission. Tunbridge Wells was such a base. Generally there was only one priest per Mission, but in the case of Tunbridge Wells, there seems to have been about two-three in residence during the first three years, probably overlapping their appointments. It may be that this new Mission was thought to deserve more attention than normal.

Its first priest was Fr. Randall Lythgoe, SJ. (1838-40 in Tunbridge Wells) who seems to have been on his own for the first year. He was joined by two other Jesuits, a Lancastrian Fr. Charles Lomax (1839-40) and Fr. James Knight (1839-40), but all three of them moved on during 1840, Fr. Lythgoe to become head of the English Province of the Jesuits. They were replaced by another Lancastrian, Fr. William Rowe (1840-41), who would return to Tunbridge Wells for two further periods (1845-51 and 1855-60) – serving a total of 12 years in Tunbridge Wells. It would seem that from 1841 St. Augustine's was down to an establishment of just one priest who would stay for 4-6 years. A Yorkshireman, Fr. William Waterton took over for four years from 1841-1845 and then there were two Irish Jesuits, Fr.

Maurice Mann (1851-1855) and Fr. Thomas Clarke ((1861-1866) who was the priest who 'resigned the mission' (the official term) to the Diocesan Bishop of Southwark.

THE DIOCESAN PRIESTS

Of the 10 Diocesan priests, one would serve the Parish for 46 years (although only 38 years as Parish Priest), another for 32, and three would serve for 17 years each, making an unduplicated total for the five of 113 years – over 75% of the 147 'Diocesan Parish Priest' years. It has also had five priests as Vicarius Adjutor (i.e. priest-in-charge) for a total of five years while the Parish Priest was sick. All but one of the Diocesan priests are now dead and six of them died while still carrying out their duties as Parish Priest. It is of interest, and it is thought of significance, that four of the Parish Priests (Canon Searle, Fr. Charles Stapley, Fr. Arthur Dudley, and Canon John Stephenson), as well as one Vicarius Adjutor (Father Herbert Evans) and a number of curates, were converts to Catholicism, which has contributed an extra dimension to the Parish and its life.

The first priest (Parish Priest was not yet an official title), Fr. (and later in 1888, Canon) **Joseph Searle** (1867-1899) was one of the longest serving with 32 years 'in post'. Born in 1825, Joseph Searle was the son of a London lawyer and a convert, having been received into the Church in 1852 at the age of 27. He opted for the priesthood and was ordained in 1859, went briefly to a parish in Chislehurst, and then as Chaplain to the Convent of the Society of the Holy Child Jesus (SHCJ) at St. Leonard's for six years – an experience which he later described as 'the unhappiest time of my life'. The SHCJ had been founded in 1846 by the dynamic American heiress, Mrs. Cornelia Connelly, who was also a convert to Catholicism. Her extraordinary story is not the subject of this work, but what is important is that Joseph Searle, while Chaplain, was instrumental in 1862 in getting for the SHCJ, the ruined Old Palace at Mayfield, which had been a Palace of the Archbishop of Canterbury in Catholic times, and which was up for sale. Mayfield is only 9 miles from Tunbridge Wells and would play a part in the history of St. Augustine's.

In 1866, the Jesuits felt that their missionary task in Tunbridge Wells was complete and their endeavours could be better employed elsewhere. They asked Dr. Thomas Grant, who was the first

Catholic Bishop of Southwark to take over what was still a Mission. He agreed and named Joseph Searle to take over on 6th January 1867. The prospect did not please Fr. Searle and he begged the Bishop to be excused, but the Bishop refused. The switch-over was far from amicable. The Jesuits asked the Bishop for compensation for the £4,000 which they estimated they had put into building the Mission. The Bishop, who had no money anyway, declined. But there were small practical issues, such as buying the presbytery furniture, which caused problems for Fr. Joseph Searle –'the mission is (so) destitute, that I am (already) supporting it out of my private means'. He wrote a round-robin letter (printed on fine rice paper) to his parishioners appealing for financial support, without much response.

Fr. Searle also started the tradition of having Missions, lasting a fortnight, to concentrate the minds of parishioners on their religion. Since the beginning, they have generally been run for the Parish by the Redemptorist Fathers. The first was in 1868, the second in 1874 and the third in 1877. More recently they have been held about every 8-12 years and the most recent one was in 2012.

Apparently Joseph Searle had a 'fiery no-holds-barred tongue' which must have made him a hero to some, but not to others. Five of his sermons given between 1867 and 1882 still exist in print – copies of them were sold at the time to raise funds. He also had to battle with continuing financial problems – parish income never matched necessary expenditure and it emerged at the end of his life that he had been subsidising the parish from his own private income, as was to be the case with at least one other Parish Priest.

Fr. Searle also conducted the very first burial ever in the new Hawkenbury Cemetery just opened by the Tunbridge Wells Commissioners in 1873, when he buried Isabella Mary Burrows of Culverden Lodge, a Catholic widow aged 32, on 14th October,1873.

In 1884, Fr. Searle celebrated the 25th Anniversary of his ordination and his parishioners showed their appreciation by giving him £100 in gold sovereigns in a silk purse. This was a considerable amount of money in those days – equivalent to a significant proportion of the Parish's Annual Income. With this money, he started his next project, a campanile with clock and carillon for the church. This would potentially coincide with both Queen Victoria's Golden

Jubilee in 1887 and the Church's own 50th Anniversary in 1888. Joseph Searle's work was rewarded when he was appointed a Canon of the Diocese in 1888. Canon Searle was also given a silk purse of £217 in gold in 1892, on the occasion of his 25th Anniversary as the Rector.

The Canon had a very good and close friend in Benedetto Bianchi, an Italian watchmaker and jeweller who had fled to England in 1860 when Garibaldi attacked Rome. Bianchi had opened a shop in Grosvenor Road next to St. Augustine's Presbytery and would be responsible for maintaining the clock and bells. He was also party to a subterfuge which was quite common in the 19th century when the Church wanted to buy a property, particularly if it was at auction. Because anti-Catholic feeling was still strong, even if it was only among a minority, it was felt to be more discreet to have the property acquired by a third-party, who was a Catholic and who would then sell it on to the Church. This is what happened in 1888 when Mr. Bianchi bought Brunswick Villa, which was adjoining St. Augustine's boundary, in Hanover Road. It cost £1,200, of which the Bishop could only loan £270.18s.7d, which left over £900 on mortgage at 5%. This debt was to prove a major headache for the parish, however the acquisition of the property was a major benefit since the site would in due course be essential for the expansion of St. Augustine's Primary School.

The Canon had one last project which he hoped to achieve, which was to have the Church consecrated, an act which is only possible in Canon Law if the Church as such (not necessarily the Parish) is free from debt. Sadly the consecration did not take place until five years after his death.

Father Charles Stapley (PP 1900-1906) was very different from the Canon, although like the Canon, he was also a convert. Known to his clerical colleagues as 'Charlie', he was tubby, bald, and an extrovert with a great sense of humour. He loved a good joke, a good cigar and a good whisky and he preached a good sermon - without any notes. He was born at Bexhill in 1853, the eldest of nine children of a veterinary surgeon. He became a vet like his father. During his Veterinary College studies, he became a Catholic and set up his veterinary practice in Eastbourne. But he suddenly gave up his practice to one of his younger brothers and went off to Paris and Valladolid to train for the priesthood, returning to England to be ordained. He was sent to the Church of Our Lady and St. Philip in Arundel which had been opened in 1873 (it is now the Cathedral for the Arundel & Brighton Diocese) where he was also unofficially chaplain to the Duke of Norfolk and got to know the family sufficiently well that he was invited every year to spend his summer holiday at the Castle. He asked for a transfer and was sent to Wandsworth, then Mark Cross, and then in 1890 to Eastbourne and then in 1894 to Deptford, where he stayed three years before posted to Tunbridge Wells in 1897 to assist the ageing Canon Searle. He succeeded the Canon in 1900. His six years as Parish Priest were short, but momentous.

His real achievement was in bringing to fruition Canon Searle's dream of making Tonbridge a separate parish with its own church and resident priest. However this achievement was to cripple St. Augustine's financially for many years to come – the money borrowed, the debts incurred, would be a halter around the parish's neck. The situation was compounded in 1905 when the schoolroom in the crypt under the Church, which had been opened only 18 years previously, was condemned for use and the grant from the Local Authority was withdrawn. So clearly a new school needed to be built, which it was by the next Parish Priest.

Canon James Keatinge (1854-1923; PP 1906-1923)

Canon James Keatinge who took over from Father Stapley was a man who has been said to be 60 years ahead of his time – that is, 60 years ahead of Vatican II – since he has been described as the 'perfect ecumenist'. An extrovert with a sharp brain and a great personality, he was very methodical, kept meticulous records and had sound judgment.

He came from a comfortably-off Catholic family whose three sons and one daughter all entered religious life. He was the eldest, born in 1854, and was ordained in 1877. His younger brother Charles, born 1857 and ordained in 1885, and his youngest brother William, born 1869 and ordained in 1893, were both to become Military Chaplains, with William rising during the First World War to be the most senior Catholic chaplain, with the rank of Chaplain-General (equivalent to Brigadier-General) and the post of Bishop of the

Forces and Titular Bishop of Metellopolis. Both brothers were to be frequent visitors to St. Augustine's and took part in the life of the parish. Fr. Charles was actually acting as his brother's curate when he died in Tunbridge Wells in 1906 at the age of 49, and the Bishop continued to be known familiarly by all the parishioners as 'Fr. Willie', long after he was raised to his Bishopric. Fr. Willie died in 1934, aged 65.

Fr. James (as he then was) started his clerical career at Arundel, then was transferred to Southwark Cathedral and then to Chatham. In 1892, he was recalled to the Cathedral as Administrator. His fund-raising and administrative skills raised him to the title of Canon in 1895 and he remained Administrator until 1904 when he took on the parish of Sutton, but only for a year, since Bishop Amigo decided to send him to Tunbridge Wells, warning him that he would find ' a bankrupt church, a house in ruins and a school condemned'.

Canon Keatinge made a very energetic start. He had been a great friend of Charlie Stapley and he cheerfully inherited a daunting situation and with the help of his brothers and his own administrative skills, he brought the financial situation under control.

The debt on the Church itself was eliminated so that it could at last be consecrated by Bishop Peter Amigo of Southwark in 1906. To mark this occasion, the Church was redecorated and electricity was installed to replace the gas jets; and new heating was installed.

A school debt Sinking Fund was established separately to pay for the new school on the site of Brunswick Villa beside the Church. It was built in 1907, cost £1,500 and had three classrooms, two of them with sliding doors which opened up to make a parish meeting room of all three. Some 25 Founder subscribers paid £10 or more *a year* and this raised £161 *a year*, but the other 400 parishioners gave less than £16, so it would take some years for the debt to be eliminated.

In 1911, he wrote that the annual parish income was only £400, but the expenditure was £695, and although he had been subsidising the parish 'from my own slender resources' to the tune of £4 a week, the parish debt had risen to £1,195 in five years and that he was now at the end of his resources – 'my purse is empty'. Such had been the situation for his two predecessors. Indeed 'they had died bankrupt...Such an ending I would fain avoid.'

Canon Keatinge had also inherited Mrs. Fenwick (more of her saga in Chapter 7) but she died in 1915 and so he was released from that worry. But other worries arose with the start of the First World War in August 1914. One complete Belgian village with its Mayor took refuge in Tunbridge Wells. They were accommodated mainly in three empty mansions, and as co-religionists it fell to St. Augustine's to give particular assistance.

Canon Keatinge was delighted with the arrival of the Sacred Heart nuns at Beechwood in Pembury Road in 1915. Not only did it mean stipends for saying Mass and other Offices for them, but it also meant that they could be involved in the Parish. That year the Parish was able to hold its first open-air Corpus Christi procession in the rhododendron-studded garden of the Convent – the first of many to come.

A typical Corpus Christi procession at the Sacred Heart Convent, held over many years.

Canon Keatinge was not a well man in the last five years of his life to the extent that in this period no less than six priests acted short-term as Vicarius Adjutor (i.e. priest-in-charge, with full responsibility for the administration of the parish) for him. He wrote to the Bishop in June 1922 saying that his health was so poor that he thought that it was time he handed over the reins to a younger man. The bishop replied sympathetically, but refused his request, writing "you have always been excellent in directing work and all your former curates.. praise you to the skies. This you can do in Tunbridge Wells even in a bad state of health. You have two very good curates and the parish work will not suffer under your direction, even if you leave the drudgery part altogether to them".

 What the Bishop did not know was that one of those curates was to die unexpectedly at the age of 49 at the end of October. He was **Fr. Charles Trapp**, born in Bedford, a convert, a member of the D'Oyly Carte Opera Company and a late vocation, who was ordained in 1916 and came immediately to Tunbridge Wells, where his musical skills enriched the sung liturgy, the choir and the social activities of the parish.

In view of Fr. Trapp's death and Canon Keatinge's ill health, **Fr. Herbert Massy Myddleton Evans (1860-1923)** was appointed the penultimate Vicarius Adjutor in February 1923 but he also was to die after less than two months in post. Fr. Evans was a convert clergyman who had been ordained in 1904, but his ministry had been dogged with ill-health. According to Lottie Wall, who was the parish organist for 30 years from 1904-1934, "he was a gentleman, a fine no-nonsense type who knew his own mind" and it would seem that even in the short time he was there, he fell foul of the parish 'establishment' – a group described by Ted Marchant as "upper crust parishioners who, by virtue of the fact that they could afford to sit at Mass (*the pew rent system was still in force*), thought that they had the right to rule the Church." Besides Lottie the organist, he had only one friend – his Irish wolfhound who was found dead in the presbytery garden and he told Lottie "they've poisoned my dog". He died shortly afterwards at the end of March, some said hounded to his grave.

Another Vicarius Adjutor, **Fr. George Boniface**, was then appointed in early May 1923, who would become Parish Priest just four months later when Canon Keatinge died at the beginning of September 1923. Fr. Boniface would remain Parish Priest until his own death in February 1940 at the age of 66. Fr. Boniface was a person about whom there are many conflicting reports and opinions. Born in Hastings, he was ordained in 1900 and ministered in parishes in Balham, Frimley and Greenwich, before he became an Army Chaplain in April 1915 and was sent to Gallipoli where he suffered from dysentery and malaria and was invalided out of the Army in October 1916. He was sent as Chaplain to the SHCJ Convent at Mayfield until March 1920, when he was transferred to Newington, staying there until appointed Vicarius Adjutor in Tunbridge Wells in 1923.

Fr. Boniface was a tall white-haired man who was aged beyond his years. He was soon adored by his poorer parishioners because he was extremely kind and generous and was a man of the people. But he had a problem – a drink problem, probably created by his War experience - which seems to have been intermittent. It was a problem which caused great offence among certain parishioners, one of whom shouted at him 'you're drunk, Sir' when he was on the altar. In 1934, antagonism escalated between a staunch but disapproving Catholic, William Vinehill, who had jet-black hair, waxed moustache, a perpetual winged collar and was virtually a teetotaller (except for a glass of sherry at Christmas), and who had been the verger for 42 years, and Fr. Boniface, which led to Fr. Boniface dismissing him as verger. The dismissal was not accepted and it led to the police being called to eject the verger after an unholy chase around the church during High Mass. As William Vinehill was the Circulation Manager of the Kent & Sussex Courier, it was almost inevitable that the conflict was reported in the newspaper for several weeks.

But there is no doubt that Fr. Boniface did a great deal of good in the parish. He helped set up a branch of the Catholic Women's League in 1924, which led to the formation of the Union of Catholic Mothers and the Girl Guides. In 1926 the Guild of the Blessed Sacrament was set up, in 1930 a Social Guild and Brotherhood and in 1933 a Boys' Club. The Centenary of St. Augustine's Church was celebrated on 17th July 1938 when Archbishop Amigo, who had been the Archbishop of Southwark for the previous 25 years, came and celebrated Mass.

Fr. Boniface died suddenly in February 1940, aged 66. A long cortege followed his coffin to Hawkenbury Cemetery and as a sign of the respect and admiration in which he was held by most, an imposing 10-ft granite Celtic Cross was erected by public subscription over his grave in 1942.

Canon Edward Fennessey (1883-1953; PP 1940-1945) took over the Parish one month after Fr. Boniface's death. He was no stranger to the Parish having served twice before. He was born in 1883, entered the Seminary at the age of 14 and was ordained at 25. He served five years as a curate in Bermondsey before coming to Tunbridge Wells at the beginning of 1914. But he was restless. He left to study at Cambridge but only stayed five months and returned to Tunbridge Wells at the end of February 1915. He was then made Rector at Mitcham in 1916 where he stayed until 1923, when he was appointed Diocesan Secretary at Bishop's House, a post he held for eight years. From there he went as Parish Priest to Sutton Park, near Guildford, for ten years, being made a Canon in 1935.

Canon Fennessey was a short, precise man with gold-rimmed glasses and it would seem that the strain of running the Parish in wartime took its toll of him. His nerves were shattered and he gave up just three weeks before the end of the War. To the astonishment of his congregation, he told them on 15th April 1945 that he would be leaving in three days' time to take up the much smaller parish of Wadhurst. However he only lasted ten months there and the rest of his life was effectively semi- and full retirement.

The War produced some unusual events for him and the Parish, such as the Special Branch arrests of 'enemy' aliens while he was saying Mass; and the bomb which landed in Grosvenor Road just outside the Presbytery, but these are reported in more detail elsewhere in this history (Chapter 8).

Fr. Arthur Dudley (1890-1949; PP 1945-1949) took over the Parish a day after Canon Fennessey left. He was an Anglican parson who converted to Catholicism and went to the Beda College in Rome, where he was ordained in 1916. His first posting was to Lewisham but after seven months he transferred to the Cathedral as a curate. In 1921 he was posted to Eastbourne for five years and then he was appointed temporary Parish priest at Dorking and then Norbury.

Bishop Amigo had been concerned for some time about reaching Catholics who lived miles from a church and who went infrequently or never to Mass. Consequently the Bishop and Fr. Dudley conceived the idea of the Travelling Mission. For two years Father Dudley fanned out from his base at West Grinstead to visit by car

some 16 centres which he founded, to say Mass for some 768 Catholics - he was very meticulous in recording the details. He was given an assistant priest, Fr. Bayliss, to help but the strain of the work still caused Fr. Dudley to have a breakdown. When he recovered, he was made Rector of Goudhurst in 1931 and stayed five years before being posted to Molesey and then onto Arundel, where like Fr. Stapley before him, he was both Parish Priest and Chaplain to the Duke of Norfolk. In April 1945 he arrived in Tunbridge Wells to take over from Canon Fennessy.

He was to have only four years at St. Augustine's and the last year was marred by his having a stroke, but Fr. Dudley's contribution to the Parish was to introduce the idea of the Travelling Mission which would lead to the foundation of the parishes of Southborough and Pembury and Mass Centres in other remote parts of the Parish. Initially, services were held on alternate Sundays in the Victoria Hall at Southborough, the Oast House in Pembury and Hamsell Manor in Eridge.

Fr. Dudley had a great devotion to the Blessed Sacrament and in 1947, possibly because he had the assured confidence of an ex-Anglican, decided that the Corpus Christi procession, usually held in the grounds of the Sacred Heart Convent, should go through the streets of Tunbridge Wells itself, carrying the Faith to the outside world. The event was delayed that year for two weeks by rain, but the procession through the Town was repeated the following year.

Fr. Dudley died peacefully in April 1949. His successor was already in place in the person of Fr. John Stephenson, who had been drafted in as Vicarius Adjutor during Fr. Dudley's first illness in 1947.

Fr. (later Canon) John Stephenson (1892?-1967; PP 1949-1967)

"Stevie", as Fr. Stephenson was popularly yet respectfully called, was born in Durham, started work as a miner at the age of 14, but was quickly found unsuitable and was given the opportunity to study and take exams which led him to London. He started to study for the Anglican priesthood but when the First World War began, he joined the 8th Battalion, Durham Light Infantry and was commissioned, rising to the rank of Captain. He won the Military Cross (MC) at the Battle of the Somme. On being demobbed, he continued his studies, obtaining a BA from London University and was ordained at Chelmsford Cathedral in 1925. For the next 20 years, he was an Anglican priest in charge of two parishes in Camberwell, where he got to know Bishop Peter Amigo.

When he decided to become a Catholic, he spent a short time at Downside School and Prinknash Abbey and then went to the Beda College in Rome, being ordained at St. John Lateran in 1947 at the age of 55. On his return, Bishop Amigo sent him as a curate to the Catholic church in his old area, Camberwell, for three months until Fr. Dudley was taken ill, when he was drafted to Tunbridge Wells as Vicarius Adjutor.

He had a difficult task, being appointed over two curates already in situ – Fr. Arthur Woolmer and Fr. Anthony Cunningham. In April 1948, Fr. Dudley had a severe stroke and a year later he died. Fr. Stephenson then put into operation two plans he had been preparing, building a new school and setting up Mass Centres to make it easier for the vast majority of the congregation who did not have cars. The first Mass Centre opened in Southborough in 1950, the new School was going to take a bit longer. He also acquired a housekeeper – Mrs. Lilian McGuire, a widow, whose son lived in Tunbridge Wells. (See page 74-75).

During the 1950s, the Parish grew considerably. Average Mass attendance increased from about 700 in 1949 to 1,500 in 1962, baptisms were up from about 80 to 120, weddings from under 20 to nearly 60. Fr. Stephenson took it in his stride, helped by some very competent curates. One in particular, Fr. Nigel Larn (see page 106) played a major part in getting the new school for St. Augustine's under way. He was however to leave in 1959 when the Primary School had been largely achieved, but the Secondary School was still being fought for. He was replaced as senior curate by Fr. Bill Howell. The Parish was very fortunate in getting him, since about this time, Fr. Stephenson who was nearly 70 began to have ill-health which became progressively worse, to the extent that Fr. Howell was appointed Vicarius Adjutor in April 1964. Fr. Stephenson was to die in August 1967, much loved by his Parish and cared for to the end by his devoted housekeeper, 'Mrs. Mac'.

Fr. William Howell (1925-2009; came to Tunbridge Wells 1959, PP 1967-1995) was the longest-serving priest (36 years) in the Parish's history, coming as the 'senior' curate in 1959, then serving as Vicarius Adjutor from 1964 until appointed Parish Priest in

1967. Fr. Bill, as he was known by everybody, was a Scot by origin and aged 34 when he arrived. He had just spent five years as a Chaplain in the Royal Navy, serving mainly the Mediterranean fleet. He was young, jaunty, care-free, confident, open-minded and his congregation warmed to him. He was full of new ideas. He abolished the second collection at the end of Sunday Mass, although it would return ten years later, as a collection *after* Mass to help the Building Fund for the new Church and would subsequently become the Outreach Collection (see page 94-95). He started with the help of his Committee the monthly Parish magazine 'The Augustinian'. He also led his Parish into becoming 'the caring church'. This was the time of Vatican II when the Catholic Church was shedding its 19th century autocratic and authoritarian image and becoming much more democratic, human and understanding; and much more ecumenical. Fr. Bill was in the vanguard of this.

In 1963 Prince Philip had launched his 'Freedom from Hunger' campaign and the Mayor of Tunbridge Wells launched an appeal for £10,000 and St. Augustine's committed itself to raising £300. In the event, it raised £809. This led to the very successful 'Marumba' project (see pages 92-93) which would lead to increased involvement by the Parish in the Third World.

Fr. Bill was a very hospitable person and his hospitability led to the development of visits to the Parish by priests from overseas – in all, over 30 priests participated in our Parish life between 1960 and 1970, often for only a week or two but sometimes for longer, and it helped the Parish and its congregation to acquire a more international and cosmopolitan approach to Christianity and Catholicism worldwide. (See pages 48-49 and the list of visiting priests in Appendix 2.) Unfortunately, visiting priests ceased with the 8 year hiatus between the demolition of the Church in Hanover Road and its successor in Crescent Road being built, and the numbers never picked up again.

Fr. Bill led the Parish through what was the most traumatic period of its history – the acceptance that the historic church in Hanover Road needed to be replaced because it was too small for its congregation; and the trauma of finding an alternative site and funding and building a new church. His leadership was a total success and he would continue 'in post' for another 20 years. However when he reached the age of 70 (five years later than what was then the usual retirement age for priests), he asked to be given a smaller, less demanding parish as a step towards retirement and this request was agreed.

A pamphlet containing 28 of his inspirational sermons was published in 2009 by Lucia Crewdson and Janet Clare under the title 'Reflections from Fr. Bill'.

Fr. (later Canon and Bishop) Michael Evans (1951-2011; PP 1995-2003) The son of a Welsh father and a French mother, he was ordained in 1975 and studied for a Master of Theology degree at the University of London from 1975-1979, subsequently returning to St. John's Seminary, Wonersh, for eight years as a lecturer in Doctrine, and then as Vice-Rector.

In 1995 he was appointed as Parish Priest at St. Augustine's Church. He is on record as saying several times that he would have preferred to have been appointed to a poor East End parish but nonetheless he threw himself into his new role with his customary vigour. He was in modern parlance a 'workaholic', working early in the morning and late into the night and doing all sorts of jobs, including being Co-Secretary of the British Methodist/ Catholic Committee. He was particularly keen on encouraging youth involvement in the Parish since he said that they were the future of the Church. The 9.30am Sunday Mass which he encouraged as a Family Mass, was in his own words 'organised chaos'. He was also responsible for building the new Parish Hall complex in 2001 and was the driving force behind the Parish's involvement in Cambodia and its 'twinning' with the Parish of Kompong Thom (see pages 93-94).

He was appointed a Canon of the Diocese in 2001 and in February 2003 Pope John Paul II appointed him as the third Bishop of East Anglia in succession to the Most Rev. Peter Smith, who had become Archbishop of Cardiff in 2001, and who became subsequently Archbishop of Southwark in 2011. Canon Michael was ordained Bishop on 19 March 2003.

In November 2006 Bishop Michael told his Diocese that he had prostate cancer. He wrote "Rather than resign, I would like to continue among you as your bishop and the father of our diocesan family until this stage of my life ends. I do not know how long that will be."

Bishop Evans died nearly five years later on 11 July 2011, aged 59. A humble man. A great man. St. Augustine's is privileged to have had him as their pastor for eight short years.

**Fr. (later Canon) Peter Stodart (1947 - to date; PP 2003 - to date).** Born in Hastings, Fr. Peter as he prefers to be known, was brought up in Gravesend and Lewisham and went to school at St. Mary's Grammar School, Sidcup. Before deciding to try his vocation, he worked as a computer programmer. When he was 24, he went to St. John's Seminary, Wonersh for six years and was ordained in June 1977 at his family's parish church, St. Saviour's, Lewisham. He was an Assistant Priest at St. Francis, Maidstone from 1977-1982; at St. George's Cathedral from 1982-1988; and Our Lady of the Annunciation, Addiscombe from 1988-1992. He became Parish Priest of Our Lady of the Annunciation, Addiscombe in 1992 before being moved in 2003 to be Parish Priest of St. Augustine's, Tunbridge Wells. He is the Dean of St. Augustine's Deanery within the Archdiocese and was made a Canon of the Diocese in 2012.

ASSISTANT PRIESTS

Although the first Assistant Priest (or curate, as they were known in those days), Fr. James Walsh, was not appointed until 1894, St. Augustine's has benefitted from the ministrations of at least 65 Assistant Priests during the 119 year interval. Many of them have been young priests, often straight out of the Seminary, who have stayed a relatively short time - 2-4 years – to gain experience before being promoted to more senior and possibly more arduous posts. In recent times, it is clear that the Bishop has often viewed the posting as a gentle introduction for new priests to the rigours of parish life.

While in recent years the norm has been two Assistant Priests, staffing in earlier years was much as five Assistant Priests, mainly due to the wider boundaries of the Parish and the need to provide priests to say Mass in places which were not then independent, such as Tonbridge, Pembury, Paddock Wood and Southborough, and also at the Mass Centres which then existed in Rusthall, Sherwood, Ramslye and Penshurst,

All the 65 Assistant Priests will be found listed in Appendix 1, with the dates of their service where known. Regrettably the Parish Archives are not as detailed as might be hoped and so there are some about whom little is known. There is also not room in this short history to go into much detail, but nonetheless a thumbnail sketch is given below of some of the more notable or well-known ones.

Fr. Charles Trapp (d.1922) [1917-1922] –see this Chapter, page 38.

Fr.Desmond Coffey (1895-1977) [1929-33] was extremely musical and made Plain Chant his life. He founded a Plain Chant Choir & Society in the parish, and in doing so, came up against the established Church Choir run for 30 years by Lottie Wall, the church organist, who disapproved of Plain Chant. He encouraged Miss Cosgrove of St. Augustine's School to enter her pupils in the Tunbridge Wells Musical Festival and they swept the board. He organised a Massed Choir Festival at St. George's Cathedral, Southwark in 1931 and entered both St. Augustine's School and the Sacred Heart Convent choirs, whom he had trained. The result was a tie for 1st place. In 1936, he conducted the Massed Choirs at the Eucharistic Congress held in Wembley Stadium.

Fr. Albert (Dick) Tomei (1906-1975) [1941-44] Born in Anerley, he entered the Seminary at the age of 16, and studied at the English College in Rome, where he got a Ph.D and was ordained in 1932. Known to his fellow priests as 'Dick', he was described as 'brilliant', 'instantly likeable' but 'highly nervous', but he gave a fine sermon. He was Archbishop Amigo's Secretary for two years but became ill and went as a curate to West Croydon, coming to Tunbridge Wells in 1941 to replace another curate, Fr. Leach, who had died suddenly at the age of 39. After three years, he returned to Croydon for another six, before going to be Rector to Carshalton Beeches, where he remained until his death in a car accident in 1975.

Fr. Nigel Larn [1954-59] – see Chapter 9, page 106.
Fr. Bernard Hegarty (d.1979)[1956-68] – see Chapter 6, pages 60-61 and Chapter 9, pages 106-7.
Fr. Hugh Clarke (1920-2007). Born in Dublin, he came with his mother to Tunbridge Wells when he was one year old. Attended St. Augustine's School, was an Altar server under Alfred Hubble, and

went to Mayfield College, and then to the Junior Seminary at Mark Cross and then to Wonersh where he was ordained in 1945. He then went to Cambridge to read History for four years and then to teach at St. John Fisher School in Purley. He was a frequent visitor to Tunbridge Wells at major feasts 'to help out'. He then became a Carmelite at Aylesford, and was their Prior for some time.

Fr. (John) Hugh Ryan (1908-90) [1970-90]. A Josephite Father, who came to St. Augustine's in a 'supply' capacity and then spent 18 years of retirement here as an assistant priest. Much loved by the parishioners as 'a character' and for his warm nature and also his interest in beer-brewing. He joined the Josephite Fathers at Weybridge, studied French at King's College, London from 1927-30 and then obtained his Licentiate é Lettres (L-é-L) and Baccalaureate in Thomistic Theology at Louvain University. He was ordained in 1936, obtained his Teaching Diploma in 1939 and returned to St. George's College, Weybridge to teach. In due course he became Headmaster of the College until he retired in 1970 and came to Tunbridge Wells.

Fr. Matthew Dickens [1994-2000] A Cambridge graduate and a convert, he was ordained in 1994 and appointed to St. Augustine's. In 2000, he was made the Parish Priest of St. Gertrude's, South Croydon and then the Parish Priest of Northfleet; and is now the Vicar-General of the Archdiocese and a Monsignor.

Thumbnail portraits of Assistant Priests who have served the Parish in the last ten years have been deliberately excluded from this history, since it is felt that their inclusion would be intrusive.

OTHER PRIESTS
It should also be recorded that the Parish has benefitted from the services of many other priests who 'visited' often over quite a long period, or with a regular frequency.

These included Army Chaplains and Belgian and French 'refugee' priests in both the First and Second World Wars.

More recently, particularly in the 1950s and 1960s, at least 36 priests from all over the world (who are listed in Appendix 2) came to visit for two to four weeks, generally acting in a 'Supply' capacity while studying in the UK or Rome. It was an arrangement which suited everybody. The visiting priests had a holiday in a pleasant place, often getting good practice with their English while the Tunbridge Wells priests had the opportunity for a break. The practice had grown in the 50s and 60s probably due to the friendly and hospitable nature of both Fr. Stephenson and Fr. Howell. However it largely died out when the Church in Hanover Road was demolished and the priests' accommodation would be severely limited for over eight years until the new Church was built in Crescent Road.

DEACONS
St. Augustine's has also been blessed in recent years by having had three Deacons in its service.

The first was Noel Lewenz who was married to Phyllis, served in the Army for 20 years and then came to St. Augustine's where he was ordained a Deacon and served from 1981-1992, dying in 1994 at the age of 79.

The second is Kevin Dunne, a parishioner of long-standing who became a Deacon in 1988 and is still serving the parish most ably, with the devoted assistance of his wife, Jean, who is also the Parish Sacristan. He will celebrate the 25th Anniversary of his ordination in 2013.

The third is Donald Coleman (familiarly known as Don), an unmarried parishioner who became a Deacon on his retirement in 1995 and was subsequently ordained a priest in 2006, becoming the parish priest of Birchington in Kent, but retired in 2012.

CHAPTER 5   THE SIZE OF THE PARISH

The Parish has grown in numbers from approximately 50 in 1838 to about 7,800 in 2012, while at the same time the area of the Parish, as defined by its boundaries, has shrunk considerably. A number of new parishes have been born within those boundaries and become separate and independent, but the congregation of this diminishing parish has still grown despite this.

In the 19th century, it was very difficult indeed for Catholics to attend Mass. There were relatively few Catholic churches, although their number was increasing steadily, and the vast majority of Catholics had no means of transport. Nonetheless it was not unusual for *devoted* Catholic families (adults and children) to walk 5-10 miles to Mass on Sundays – roughly 2-4 hours in each direction – to attend. Less devoted Catholics would obviously *and understandably* have made such a journey less often. However it should also be recognised that, both then and now, there has always been a significant difference between the number known to be or declaring themselves to be Catholics; and the number who actually attend Mass on a Sunday, as is their theoretical bounden duty as a Catholic.

For the first 80 years or so, there was no *regular* reporting of parish statistical information. The Bishop (or Archbishop) has always made a Visitation every 2-3 years to every parish and before that occurs, the Rector or Parish Priest answers a standardised Visitation Form which provides statistical and other information about the parish so that the Bishop can assess better the parish during his Visitation. This form was never intended to be part of a wider Diocesan overview, nor a part of a parish statistical database, although it would be realised in due course that both of these were needed.

In 1898, Canon Searle reported to the Archbishop that there were 488 Catholics in the Tunbridge Wells area (which still included Tonbridge) out of a population of 61,240 (i.e. only 0.8%); and that

313 were 'practising their faith', however that was defined. The School had 101 pupils, not all of them Catholic.

Statistical procedures and techniques have gradually been introduced. There is still in the Parish Archives a red-bound Index which states that it is a Census begun on the 16th March 1911 by Canon James Keatinge. It is not a census as we would know it today, but is a quite chatty alphabetical record of the members, including their addresses, family size, financial situation, and their diligence and (some of) their foibles. As a record, it has also clearly been added to, by subsequent incumbents. More statistical Censuses have been conducted in the Parish in later years, including one in 1964, which defined the Catholic population as 3,385, but also provided (amongst others) a Table showing how many of them read Catholic newspapers and with what frequency. (For the curious reader, the answers are 23% regularly, 45% sometimes, 19% never and 12% gave no reply.)

Since about 1920, every parish has to submit Annual Returns to the Diocese, enumerating the numbers attending Mass, being converted, baptised, making their First Communion, being confirmed, being married or being buried. This data provides a fascinating portrait of the Parish over time. It is complex and for the more statistically-minded it has been assembled as a Table in Appendix 3. For the more general reader, that table can be summarised as follows:

Size of Congregation. During its first 90 years, the parish grew from about 50 in 1837 to 750 by 1925 and then more than doubled to 1,800 by 1945. From 1945-60, it went up another 166% to 4,800. It is clear that accurate statistics were not available from 1960-90 and the declared size of the Congregation was generally entered each year as 4-4,500, which can only have been at best a 'guesstimate'. With the advent of computers however, much more accurate records of those calling themselves Catholic have been possible; and this has led to a database which has the names and addresses of some 7,805 Catholics within the Parish in 2012. Such a huge increase can only be explained by two factors: there must have been an under-recording of the number of Catholics in the previous 10-20 years; and the arrival in recent years in Tunbridge Wells of many immigrants from what are predominantly Catholic countries/areas, such as Poland, the Czech Republic, the Philippines, and Kerala in India. However it must also be recorded that in this period, average Mass attendance on a Sunday has dropped from 1,281 in 1990 and 1,241 in 2000 to 908 in 2012, so attendance by these *additional* Catholics at regular church services must be relatively low.

Converts are always welcome. By definition, they bring an interest, an involvement and a commitment to the Church which is often missing among the more complacent 'born Catholics'. They have contributed significantly to the life and development of the Parish and also the Church. The numbers of converts has fluctuated every year, but they seem to average about 10 a year (the 49 recorded in 2012 must be largely due to the influx from St.Barnabas).

Baptisms have also fluctuated over time from a low of 32 in 1925 to a high of 104 in 1945, which must have been the effect of war, and seem to have been between 57-75 every year from 1970 to 2010. The Catholic population has of course expanded during this time, so the figures must reflect proportionately a declining birth rate.

First Communions. Somewhat surprisingly, First Communion data was not collected until after 1960, but it shows a fairly steady rate of between 58-77 a year between 1980-2010.

Confirmations. In the past, confirmations only took place every two-three years since the Sacrament could only be given by a Bishop and they did not visit a parish every year. Now since Vatican II, the rules have been relaxed and it can be given by a priest, although many still prefer to receive the Sacrament from a Bishop. It is therefore difficult to draw any firm conclusions from the Confirmation figures in Appendix 3.

Marriages. There has been a decline in the number of marriages in St. Augustine's since 1970, which was the peak year with 35 marriages. Recently there have been only 10-15 a year, and in 2012 there were only 9. This mirrors the UK national pattern where living together without getting married, seems to have become the norm. It is interest to note from the data in Appendix 3 that historically the majority of marriages in St. Augustine's have been 'mixed' marriages i.e. between a Catholic and a non-Catholic; and that this majority has fluctuated between 66% and 90%. Only in recent years when the total number of marriages has dropped considerably, has the proportion of 'mixed' marriages dropped even more, to about 30-40%, which reflects what must be less pressure being put on the non-Catholic partner by the Catholic partner to get married in church.

It should be recognised that 'mixed marriages' have an 'upside' and a 'downside' for the Church: they can bring the non-Catholic partner into the Church; equally they can lead to the Catholic partner losing the will to remain in the Church.

Interestingly, immigrants seem to have virtually no effect on St. Augustine's marriage figures. While a number of them go through the Church's required marriage preparation course, virtually all of them very understandably choose to get married in their home town or village, whether that is Poland, the Czech Republic, India or the Philippines.

Deaths, which means essentially funerals, have only been recorded since about 1960 and insofar as it is the only unavoidable event in one's life, the data can only reflect the growth in the Catholic population and also the importance, *or otherwise*, which that Catholic population attaches ' to going to meet their Maker' in a proper fashion.

Average Mass Attendance is a slightly tricky statistic, since it is only an average of a 3-4 week sampling period during the whole 52; that period has changed over time for no doubt good reasons, from before Easter, to after Easter, to May and to October; and consequently comparisons could be challenged in terms of strict statistical validity. Nonetheless we have no other data and as such it is still very enlightening. In simple terms, Average Mass Attendance increased from 100 in 1851 to just under 500 in 1925, then grew to about 900 in the 1940s and then doubled to over 1,800 in 1960. Since then it has dropped to a relatively stable figure of about 1,250 over the twenty years 1980-2000, but then has fallen significantly to 908 in 2012, despite a considerable increase in Tunbridge Wells in the Catholic population over the last 10-20 years.

The statistics for the Catholic Population and Average Mass Attendance are clearly correlated. For one to be going up while the other is going down, needs an explanation which is beyond the scope of this present work. Obviously, Catholics from abroad may find services in English too difficult to understand or to follow; or they may have a different understanding about the requirement for a Catholic to attend Mass every Sunday. However it does not alter the fact that some (many?) Catholics from abroad do attend on a weekly basis; and so the recent decline in Average Mass Attendance must be essentially among St. Augustine's *English* congregation.

No. of Masses on a Sunday. The number of Masses offered on a Sunday, together with the number of locations offered, does have a statistical correlation with Average Mass Attendance. Flexibility of timing, coupled with ease of accessibility, does produce higher attendances.

The problem is that, with fewer priests now being available and 75% of the population owning a car, it is understandable that fewer locations can be provided/need to be serviced, or that fewer Masses can be offered. However that still leaves about 25% of Catholics who do not have a car (assuming that they conform broadly to the national average) and may be beyond reasonable accessibility.

Over the 175 years, the number of Masses offered on a Sunday has grown from 1 from 1837-1894, to 2 in 1895 and 3 in 1925 (leaving out the War years, when more were offered for the Belgians and the military). This increased to 4 in 1941 and reached 8 in 1950. With the development of Mass Centres on the periphery of the Parish boundaries during the 1950s-1960s, the number grew to 11 in 1970, of which only 4 were at St. Augustine's in Hanover Road. With the closure of Mass Centres (or their conversion into independent parishes, the total number of Masses at a weekend (Sunday including Saturday evening) has dropped to 5.

St. Augustine's Church in Hanover Road, adjoining Grosvenor Road

CHAPTER 6   NEW PARISHES AND MORE MASS CENTRES

As has been shown earlier, the boundaries of St. Augustine's have shrunk, as St. Augustine's (and others) has been instrumental in creating new and independent parishes within its old boundaries. These new parishes were very necessary, as the Parish was too large for many Catholics within it to make what would have been a long journey, particularly in the days before public transport and cars, to attend Sunday Mass, in what was the only and increasingly-too-small church in the Parish, in Hanover Road. It should be remembered that even in 1950 only 10% of households had a car and public transport on Sundays was often non-existent and car ownership was still only 20% in 1960. So the practical, physical problem of getting one's family to Mass on Sunday was a very real one for many Catholics.

In the 19th century, Mission and Parish sizes were very large because there was both a shortage of priests and a relative shortage of Catholics. But over time, the number of priests increased, as did the Catholic population, particularly from Ireland after the Potato Famine. So, two things happened.

First, new parishes were created as and when there was a sufficiently large number of Catholics in a locality to justify them and these were largely on the periphery of the Parish. Tonbridge, Southborough, and Pembury/Paddock Wood are three such parishes created within the old St. Augustine's boundaries. [10]

Second, what were called Mass Centres arose in the 1950/60s[11]. These were places where Mass was said on Sundays. Sometimes, the building belonged to the Parish, sometimes not, but they all served a number of needs – they were for some (particularly the

---

[10] It should be admitted that technically Paddock Wood was served from Tonbridge, not Tunbridge Wells, before it became a parish.

[11] The idea behind them was not new – priests had been visiting outlying parts to say Mass for a long –time, but not necessarily on a weekly basis and in a regular place. Fr. Arthur Dudley, who had originated the Travelling Mission in the 1920s with Bishop Amigo, and who was St. Augustine's PP from 1945-9, should be given credit for bringing his earlier knowledge and experience to the development of Mass Centres.

many at that time without cars), a more convenient way of attending Mass; they took some of the pressure off the Grosvenor Road Church, which was known to overflow with some of the congregation having to stand in the road to hear Mass; and with St. Augustine's at that time having as many as five priests, it was possible to establish a rota to service all the Mass Centres effectively. St. Augustine's was to have six Mass Centres, all of them at least two miles from Grosvenor Road, at Southborough, Rusthall, Ramslye, Penshurst, Sherwood, and Pembury. Two of these Mass Centres – Southborough and Pembury - would, not surprisingly, turn into independent Parishes in due course.

THE NEW PARISHES

Tonbridge

Canon Joseph Searle (Rector 1866-99) and **Fr. Charles Stapley** (Rector 1899-1906) were the two priests who between them achieved the establishment of Tonbridge as a separate parish. Canon Searle started to look for land in Tonbridge in 1887. Twice he turned down Fosse Bank near the Castle at a price of £3,500, then in 1893 he paid £925 for eight cottages in Prospect Row. His long-term intention was to demolish the cottages and build a brick or stone church but in the short-term there was room to erect on the site, at a cost of £505, a prefabricated corrugated iron church, which was put up in under two months. The Tonbridge Board only gave permission for this church to be up for 5 years. This was a quite usual restriction for such buildings in those days as they were thought to be semi-temporary, although many lasted a long time, and it did not necessarily mean that it would be pulled down in five years. The first Mass was celebrated in August 1894 and the new Church of Corpus Christi was served from St. Augustine's in Tunbridge Wells.

Canon Searle died at the end of 1899 and Fr. Stapley took over as Rector. In 1900 a resident priest, Fr. George Scott, was found for Corpus Christi, but he only stayed a year and Corpus Christi reverted to being run from St. Augustine's. The overwhelming need was to find a new site for the Church because of the five-year restriction and in August 1901 it was found in Lyons Crescent. Much land behind the High Street was as yet undeveloped and a number of plots were available at £200 a plot. Fr. Stapley selected

Plots numbered Nos. 14-17, which he got for £750, and then he added Plot No.18. The Church was designed by William Barnsley Hughes (1852-1927), who was a leading architect at the time in Tunbridge Wells, and was opened in 1904. Fr. James Walsh, who had been posted to St. Augustine's in 1899 to serve Tonbridge, was appointed in November 1904 its first rector, a post he held until his retirement twenty years later.

The funding of Corpus Christi, Tonbridge, is a complicated story involving the Marquis de Misa, a parishioner and Spanish businessman in London, and Mrs. Mary Hannah Fenwick, a North Country widow, convert and parishioner who lived in Upper Grosvenor Road. Their involvement is explained elsewhere in this history (Chapters 3 & 7).

Southborough

The foundation of the parish of St. Dunstan's, Southborough started with St. Augustine's setting up in May 1950 its first Mass Centre on Sundays in the Royal Victoria Hall, Southborough which was, and still is, an under-utilised local theatre, whose construction was funded by Sir David Salomon, MP, Mayor of Tunbridge Wells, inventor and scientist, in the late 19th century.

This Mass Centre proved so popular that it was soon looking for a permanent home, which was found at 34, London Road. It was an old house which had once been the Rectory for St. Thomas's Church in Southborough and it was sold to St. Augustine's for £4,000. Besides the two-storey house, the property included a cottage and a small hall that had been used as a classroom and now became the Chapel.

The Chapel was served by the priests of St. Augustine's until **Fr. Reginald Salter** was appointed its first resident priest in 1955. Fr. Salter was a convert who had been ordained in 1941 and spent the War as a curate in Sydenham, London. He came to Southborough from St. Leonard's and proved very popular, but he proved to be a sick man and died suddenly in 1964 after nine years in office, at the early age of 52.

He was succeeded by **Fr. Frederic Redding**, who was only at Southborough for four years, but in whose time it was resolved by the first Parish Council which he had set up, to build a Church at No.34. Plans were drawn up and presented to Tunbridge Wells Borough Council which rejected them as 'over-development'.

In 1968 Fr, Redding was moved to St. Joseph's at St. Mary Cray and he was succeeded by **Fr. (later Canon) Bernard Hegarty**, who  had been an assistant priest at St. Augustine's since 1956. Fr. Hegarty was a late vocation, having served in the Army in North Africa during the War and become a Chartered Accountant after it. His financial knowledge and experience would prove invaluable in getting the Church built. While at St. Augustine's he had been heavily involved in youth work and had sat as the Bishop's Representative on the Kent Education Committee and fought to get Catholic Schools built in Kent. He played a material part in the foundation of St. Gregory's and was loved by Catholics and others alike.

Just as he was about to take over St. Dunstan's, Fr. Hegarty was badly injured in a car crash, which his driver and parish friend, Keith Alderman, who was due to be married, sadly did not survive. On his recovery, he threw out the plans rejected by the Council and it was decided to build the Church complex in three stages – first, a large chapel-cum-hall, then the church itself and finally the priests' house. A blizzard of very successful fund-raising took place – dances, whist drives, bazaars and the 100 Club with a car as the first prize.

The Hall was built very swiftly and it was paid for by 1972. Mass was celebrated there for five years until the second stage was complete and the new Church of St. Dunstan's held its first Mass in August 1973. The new Church cost only £26,000 due to the kindness of its builder, Jack Elkington, of Elkingtons Tonbridge, who lived in Southborough and wanted to help.

In August 1975, Fr. Hegarty was 'promoted' to St. Thomas's Church in Canterbury and was made a Canon shortly afterwards. Sadly he died while on a visit to Rome in 1979.

The third stage of Southborough's development was the Presbytery which was prove much more expensive and problematic and would not be completed until 1981 at a cost of £52,000, which included two sacristies and a smaller hall beneath the Church.

Paddock Wood and Pembury

Paddock Wood: St. Justus 1949; 1950; new church 1981; consecrated 1981.)
Pembury: St. Anselm's Church and Hall. (1962; 1965)

The development of Paddock Wood and Pembury as parishes is somewhat complicated.

Paddock Wood existed as a Mass Centre served by Tonbridge before Pembury, but Pembury which was only established as a Mass Centre in 1962 and was served by Tunbridge Wells, showed such progress that it was decided to join the two as the new parish of Pembury and Paddock Wood in April 1965, with Father Nigel Larn who had been at Tunbridge Wells as its first Priest-in-charge.

In due course, because of staffing problems and with two churches to service, Paddock Wood became the dominant church serving Pembury, until the Ordinariate of Our Lady of Walsingham (*the new Ordinariate created by Benedict XVI in 2011 to allow Anglicans to enter into the full communion of the Catholic Church whilst retaining much of their heritage and traditions*) was given Pembury as a separate quasi-parish.

MASS CENTRES

The Hollies, Rusthall
St. Joseph's, Rusthall

The first Mass Centre in St. Augustine's Parish was opened in 1950 at Southborough and it was followed very quickly by Rusthall.

It had been hoped to hire the old school building beside St. Paul's Church on Rusthall Common, but this was not possible, so The Hollies, a two-storey family house at 12, Rusthall Road was bought for £4,000. The Mass Centre was established on the ground floor and the upper floor was let.

This was only a temporary measure until a brick dual-purpose hall was built in the garden. While the hall served as a church, it was called St. Joseph's, but it was also used by the Scouts who would subsequently buy it when St. Joseph's was closed in 2000 and it was sold, to become the Sunshine Hall.

The third Mass Centre was at Ramslye which was opened in 1953 in the large hall of the Primary School and would continue as a Mass Centre until 1976.

In 1962, 'The Augustinian' listed 7 Mass Centres: at Pembury Hospital, Pembury Village, the Blessed Sacrament Convent, the Sacred Heart Convent, Penshurst, Ramslye and Rusthall.

In 1981, average Mass attendance was 94 in Rusthall, 55 at Sherwood and 18 at Penshurst. In the same year, the average at St. Augustine's was 1,023, so these three Mass Centres constituted 14% of all Mass attendances.

St. Gregory's, Penshurst

Penshurst is of particular note since the Centre was in a building, built specifically as a chapel for it, in the garden of a private house, and known as St.Gregory's. Neville and Edith Cox had set up 'mini-churches' in the gardens of previous homes and so when they moved to Orchard Cottage in Penshurst, they carried on their practice. They paid for its installation and maintenance until it closed in 1982, following Neville's death in 1977 and Edith's in 1982.

In due course, Mass Centres ceased to exist. St. Joseph's in Rusthall was the last, closing in July 2000. Some have become parishes in their own right; others have closed as a combination of factors - increased car ownership (now 75% of households), a decline in vocations and therefore fewer priests to service them, and also a decline in the size of congregations – have made them less necessary, or operable.

Last Mass at Rusthall, 16th July 2000, with Fr. Michael.

Aerial view of Tunbridge Wells, in the 1920s.
Note: St. Augustine's is bottom right,
with the General Hospital above it, centre.

CHAPTER 7   THE CONGREGATION

All parishes usually have a very mixed congregation by age, sex, class and education; and today one should also add in, by nationality and ethnic origin as well.

St. Augustine's has been no different from any other parish. In the beginning, there would seem to have been a polarisation in terms of class, since the 50-odd Catholics which it served are described as being either very rich or very poor. But over time, this polarisation has diminished and the parish is now reasonably representative of the environment in which it lives. In its time, it has had French emigrés (rather than refugees) after the 1848 revolution; Belgian refugees during the First World War; a variety of refugees in the Second World War; and most recently Filipino and Polish and East European immigrants. The common thread is that they all were or are Catholics.

St. Augustine's has also had a variety of interesting parishioners – noble, rich, poor, devoted, eccentric and even dishonest – and the following is but a brief selection:

19th Century Notables

Queen Maria Amalia of Naples and Sicily (1782-1866), widow of King Louis-Philippe I of France, who was forced to abdicate in the 1848 Revolution and who came in exile with his family to England and lived for some time in Tunbridge Wells. They lived subsequently at Claremont in Surrey where she died in 1866. The Queen gave St. Augustine's the elaborate garnet-studded monstrance which was still in use until recently.

Her youngest son, **Antoine, Duc de Montpensier (1824-1890)** had married in 1846 and lived with his family mainly in Spain from 1848, where he was an unsuccessful contender for the Spanish throne in 1870. In 1870 he was provoked into a pistol duel with his cousin, the Duke of Seville, and he killed him. For this, he was convicted and sentenced to just one month in prison. In 1877 he gave

St. Augustine's the painting 'St. Anthony of Padua with the Child' (possibly by Murillo [c.1618-82], but more likely 'School of Murillo') that formed the reredos over the High Altar in the original St. Augustine's in Hanover Road. The painting has since been lost.

The Count and Countess de Bayona, and **the Marques and Marquesa de Misa** were one and the same people. **Manuel Misa y Betamati (1815-1904)** was born in Jerez, studied law and became a wine merchant who came to London in about 1845, was instrumental in setting up the Spanish Chamber of Commerce in London and was its first President. He married a Spanish cousin in 1867. He was made the 1st Count de Bayona in 1875 and the 1st Marquis de Misa in 1889[12]. The Count and Countess were the devout benefactors who paid for the construction of the Campanile in 1887; and in 1894, the Marquis de Misa lent Canon Searle £1,000 at 3½% interest towards the purchase of the first site of Corpus Christi, Tonbridge.

The Earl of Ashburnham (5th Earl, 1840-1913) lived at Ashburnham Place near Battle and owned 24,000 acres (slightly less than his neighbour, the Marquess of Abergavenny who had 30,000.) He became a Catholic in 1874 and therefore a parishioner of the extended Mission. Fr. Searle obviously 'recruited' him as a Vice-President of the Guild of St. Augustine, along with Lord William Nevill, the Count de Bayona and Mr. W.H. Bishop. The Guild seems to have been a Parish organisation, which met weekly in the winter, and of which Canon Searle was President. There is a further possible connection between the Earl and the Duc de Montpensier, who

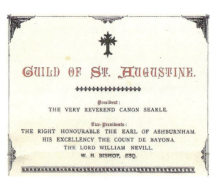

---

[12] 'Marques de Misa' is now a Spanish brandy marketed by Williams & Humbert.

was a contender for the Spanish throne, since Ashburnham was the agent in England for Don Carlos, Duke of Madrid (1848-1909), who as 'Carlos VII' was the Carlist contender for the Spanish throne from 1868. (This very tangled web has however not been unravelled by the author.)

Lord William Nevill (1860-1939) was the fourth son of the 1st Marquess of Abergavenny, who lived at Eridge Castle just three miles from Tunbridge Wells. Lord Nevill was born in 1860, educated at Eton and was a Lieutenant in the West Kent Regiment. About 1885, he was on the staff of Sir Henry Loch, the Governor of Victoria, Australia and became a Catholic there, later studying for the priesthood in Rome. His family, and particularly his father who was Low Church, was appalled. He returned to England without becoming a priest and married Luisa de Murietta, the daughter of the Marquis de Santurce, a well-known banker, just before he went bankrupt in 1896. They were not to have any children, but became parishioners of St. Augustine's, where he became the patron of a number of Church organisations.

Mr. W. H. Bishop of the White House, Culverden Down – stockbroker and financial adviser to Southwark Diocese, he was a staunch parishioner who made the presentation of 216 sovereigns in a silk purse to Canon Searle on behalf of the parish on the occasion of the 25th Jubilee of the Canon's Rectorship in Tunbridge Wells. Sadly Mr. Bishop later misappropriated Diocesan funds, gambled on the Stock Exchange and lost the Diocese thousands of pounds.

Benedetto Bianchi (see also pages 12 and 34) was an Italian watchmaker and jeweller who had fled to England in 1860 when Garibaldi attacked Rome. He must have come with money, because he bought some land in Grosvenor Road from the Church and built a row of shops next to St. Augustine's Presbytery, one of which was his jeweller's shop and above which he and his family lived. He was a church stalwart and would become a great friend of Fr. Searle. He no doubt played some part in the development of the Campanile. He certainly organised the purchase of the clock and bells and in due course would be responsible for their maintenance. He was also a key player in the subterfuge over the purchase of Brunswick Villa in 1889, which is described on pages 34.

Mrs. Mary Hannah Fenwick (1824-1915) was a generous benefactor whose benefaction would prove to be somewhat of a mixed blessing to the Parish. She was born a Protestant in 1824 and married c.1863 in Yorkshire to a husband, William, who was twelve years younger. They had one child, Walter, born in 1864.

By the 1881 Census, they had moved south to Tonbridge where they lived in Dry Hill Road but by 1887, they had moved to Cintra, No. 32, Upper Grosvenor Road, a three-storey house. Mrs. Fenwick and her son had converted to Catholicism sometime earlier, and when both her husband, who remained a Protestant, died in 1886 and her son who was disabled, died in 1887, she paid £374.15s.3d for the renovation of the crypt under the Church as a schoolroom, in their memory.

In 1899, Mrs. Fenwick, now 75, offered to give the Bishop of Southwark, Dr. Francis Bourne, later to be Cardinal Archbishop of Westminster, the sum of £5,000 for St.Augustine's and a further £2,500 to establish the Corpus Christi Church at Tonbridge. Her conditions for this gift were that she should be paid an annuity of £350 until her death; a Mass should be said for her intentions every week for as long as she lived; a further 200 Masses were to be said on her death; and an Anniversary Mass was to be said for her each year in both churches *in perpetuity*. Her offer was quickly accepted since no one thought for one moment that she would live for another 16 years. Her unexpected longevity would largely wipe out any benefit from her offer (which would at that stage have required a total annuity payment of £5,600).

The problem was however compounded further by the Bishop agreeing in 1900 to increase the annuity by another £50 (£750 over the next 15 years, bringing the cost of the annuities to £6,350), as well as promising her 50 Masses a year for her son, Walter, and an Anniversary Mass for 25 years, bringing the total number of Masses promised to at least 1,825.

Then in 1902, when she expressed her concern to the Bishop that the Corpus Christi church in Tonbridge had not yet started, he soothed her concern by writing to say that a start was about to be made and he increased her annuity by another £100, which would increase her annuity payments by another £1,300, as well as 100 Masses a year to be said for five years in Corpus Christi. The following year, with construction well in hand, Mrs. Fenwick promised a further £1,000 for Tonbridge on the same terms as before. The new Bishop of Southwark, Dr. Peter Amigo (who would remain in office until 1949) accepted, 'May God bless you for your kindness' he wrote, and offered another 150 Masses for her husband and herself (post mortem). The final straw, almost to break the camel's back, was in 1906 when he offered another £50 annuity – a further drain on the almost non-existent resources of the Mission. In all, Mrs. Fenwick gave £8,500 and received back about £7,450 in annuities, as well as at least 2,475 Masses for the repose of her soul and those of her family.

A specific problem lay in fulfilling the promises of Masses to be said. As there were only about seven Masses said at each Church each week – i.e. a total of just over 350 per church per year – and about 200 of these were committed each year to Mrs. Fenwick, the opportunity to create income for running the Parish through Mass offerings was severely limited. Canon Keatinge would later write to Bishop Amigo in 1916, saying that while he had received no stipend for saying Mrs. Fenwick's Masses, they were so numerous that he had had to pay two other priests to say them for him, at the rate of 10 Masses for a £1. As has been said earlier, Mrs. Fenwick's benevolence was a mixed blessing. It should however be recorded that Mrs. Fenwick in her Will did leave her house 'Cintra' in Upper Grosvenor Road to the Parish; and it was sold in 1918 for £763-8s-0d.

Edward Fooks was the Diocesan solicitor and gave 20 years' invaluable service as Legal Adviser to the Diocese of Southwark and to Canon Searle. He had 'piloted' Corpus Christi, Tonbridge through its 'birth' and was the Chairman of the School Debt and Maintenance Fund Committee. He lived at Langton House, Langton Green and was a partner in the London practice of Arnold, Fooks and Chadwick.

Ludwig Reich was a refugee watchmaker from Germany who came to England well before the First World War and set up shop in Camden Road. He was a pillar of the church, belonged to church societies, was a sidesman and took the collection. When the First World War began, he was briefly interned and on his return to Tunbridge Wells, the windows of his shop were smashed by xenophobic citizens and even more astonishingly, he was no longer allowed because of *parishioner* pressure, to remain a member of parish organisations, or even take the collection at Sunday Mass. The final insult was that at the end of the War, Canon Keatinge was prevented by prominent parishioners from accepting a much needed gift of £500 for the Church, which Ludwig offered as a gesture of thanksgiving for the end of the War. Disgracefully, he was never re-instated in his Church offices, but happily his business prospered after the War and he moved his shop to Monson Road, where it still is.

20th/21st Century Notables (*in alphabetical order*)

Reg & Bridget Argent. Both gave 50 years' service to the Parish, she as a sacristan, running the War on Want shop, the 'Holy' Shop, flowers for the Church, and many other charitable works. They received the Papal Benemerenti Medal in 1975,

The Card family was a part of St. Augustine's family from 1873 when grandfather Edwin served Mass for Fr. Searle and subsequently begat 14 children, of whom many played a part in the life of St. Augustine's. Principal among them was Charlie (1899-1968) who served on the Altar for 44 years. By trade, he was a bootmaker, until leg trouble forced him to become a milkman. He was a younger shadow of Alf Hubble, who came out of retirement to act as MC at his funeral, but only survived him by about a year. There were many other Cards who served the Parish – the standing joke was that the clergy always had a Card up their sleeve – including his son, Barry, his brother Edwin and cousins, Willie, Arthur and Gordon.

Laurie & Marion Clegg. On their marriage in 1959, they came to Tunbridge Wells. She taught at St. Augustine's School and was the first female Minister of the Word. Both were very active in the Parish – the Newman Circle, and Justice and Peace issues.

Eric Cockerell (d. 1990) was received into the Church in 1934 and within two months was St. Augustine's Organist and subsequently became its Choirmaster after the War. He married Alfred Hubble's daughter, Marie, in 1938 and they moved to Petts Wood. He served in the RAF during the War as an Intelligence Officer and they returned to Tunbridge Wells where he took over again the organ, which had been played in the intervening years by Eileen Ball. He retired in 1972.

Lady Gower and Pauline Gower. Lady Gower was the wife of Sir Robert Gower who was a solicitor, a Conservative Party activist and was Mayor of Tunbridge Wells from 1918-19. They lived at Sandown Court in the Pembury Road. He was knighted in August 1919, for the support he had given to a scheme for protecting businesses in their owners' absence while serving in World War I. He was elected as the MP for Hackney Central at the 1924 General Election and then in 1929 as the MP for Gillingham, a seat which he held until he retired from the Commons at the 1945 General Election.

Lady **Gower** was a Catholic and may have been a convert, as were her two daughters who attended the Sacred Heart Convent and became Catholics while there. **Pauline Gower (1910-1947)** learnt to fly at the age of 20, became one of the first women aviators, a friend of Amy Johnson, and during the Second World War was the head of the women's section of the Air Transport Auxiliary (ATA), which ferried all types of military and other aircraft around Britain. She became the first female Director of BOAC and sadly died in childbirth in 1947.

Lionel Fuller (1892-1966) and his wife, Kathleen Carey (1902-1971), were married at St. Augustine's in 1926 and were very active members and benefactors of the parish for up to 45 years. He was the President of the Catenian Association and Warden of the Guild of the Blessed Sacrament; she was very active in the Catholic Women's League at all levels – parish, diocesan and national. Both of them sang in the Church choir. They also gave very generously and anonymously of their considerable wealth, which had been made in carpets.

Alfred Hubble (1885-1969) gave 73 years' service on the Sanctuary from 1893-1966, 58 of them as MC, a position to which he was appointed at the age of 23. He ruled his sanctuary with a kindly rod and instilled such a sense of devotion that several of his 'boys' found vocations – Bishop Bernard Wall, Fr. Hugh Clarke, Fr. Tim Rice and Fr. John Chapman.

Alf's father ran the Volunteer pub in Victoria Road and Alf was educated at St. Augustine's School next to the Church until he left at the age of 12, and joined the Kent & Sussex Courier as an apprentice. He worked there for 60 years, becoming overseer of the Printing Department and retiring in August 1957. The Courier allowed him time-off for special Church events, of which the most notable was on 11th November 1918 when he rang the carillon in the Campanile for its very last time to mark the end of the Great War. He was awarded the Papal 'Benemerenti' Medal in 1955. During his service to the Church, he 'survived' seven Parish Priests and 42 Assistant Priests.

Alf Hunt (always known as Alf, never Alfred). Born 1919. Went to St. Augustine's School in 1924. An Altar Server when he was 7, in the Church Choir at 11, learning Plain Chant from Fr. Coffey, who was the first priest in the parish to have a car. Chairman of the Parish Council, Chairman of St. Gregory's Governors, Treasurer of the Parish Building Committee. First President of the SVP when it was reformed in 1964. Was one of the first Readers of the Liturgy at Mass, along with Jimmy Ludden, Brian Donovan and Hugh Reynolds.

Leo Kelly (1900-86) Born in London, he served in the Royal Navy during the First World War and married Betty Fisher (d.1998) in 1931 at St. Augustine's. They had five children – Peter, the eldest, became a White Father (now known as Missionaries of Africa) and spent most of his life in Uganda, but is now retired; Elizabeth, the second married David Watts, had four children, and both are still very active members of the Parish; and Ann the fourth who went to Africa as a nun, having joined the Franciscan Missionaries of the Divine Motherhood. Both Fr. Peter and Sr. Ann still visit St. Augustine's, when they are 'on leave'. Leo and Betty also had two other daughters, Mary who died in 2012, and Theresa, the youngest.

Leo worked for his whole career at N.M.Rothschild, the merchant bank, and became its Company Secretary. He was a pillar of St. Augustine's, advising and working (particularly on the Finance Committee) for the Parish over many years. Both he and his wife were awarded the Papal Benemerenti Medal in 1975.

Dr. William Long and family. Details about the Long family will be found on page 26. Dr. Long was so devoted to his faith that he served at Mass every morning until he was over 90.

Ted Marchant (1911-1984), the principal author of St. Augustine's first Parish history 'One Cog', published in 1995, but written by him over many years. Born in Newcastle, Ted was a third-generation journalist who started work in 1929 on provincial newspapers, moved to the Daily Mail in London after 4 years, then after a year went to the Continental Daily Mail in Paris and then became the Paris correspondent of the Daily Mirror. There he met and married his French wife, Genevieve in 1935. They had a daughter, Mirielle, in

1938 and returned to England just before the War. He served in the National Fire Service during the War, joined the Daily Sketch for three years and Reuters for eight, before returning to the Daily Mail from which he retired in 1976. His wife and daughter were lifelong Catholics, but he did not join them until 1958. Thereafter, he was very active in the Parish, being one of three MCs, and editing and producing 'The Augustinian', the monthly parish magazine/newspaper for some ten years.

Stanley Martin (1930-1987). First served on the Altar in 1936 at the age of 5½. He became the principal Parish MC after Alfred Hubble retired and was the first Special Minister of Communion at St. Augustine's in 1977. He was the Buyer at Simmonds, the Tunbridge Wells outfitters, for 14 years and Secretary of TWODS for four years.

Malcolm & Pam McCulloch – Malcolm ran all the Parish Youth Groups for many years. Pam was Parish Secretary for Fr. Bill Howell. She led the Folk Choir in the early 1980s. Ran the Holy Shop, started the Prime Timers (the group for those too young at heart to retire) and the Ladies' Lunch and Prayer Group, both of which are still thriving. She was one of the first Ministers of Holy Communion.

Mrs. Lilian McGuire (1894-1976) (or Mrs. Mac, as she was familiarly known) was Fr. Stephenson's housekeeper for over 15 years. Born in Carlisle, she was a widow whose son, daughter-in-law and grandchildren lived in Tunbridge Wells. She came to Tunbridge Wells in 1950 and applied for the job. Their relationship was a 'mother-and-son' friendship. She was his confidante, his gate-keeper, and his nurse in his last years. She ran with great efficiency a household of four priests and cooked lunch every day for as many as twelve priests.

Mrs. Phyllis Milner, Chair of CWL. A great fund-raiser and coffee morning organiser. When Phyllis returned to Calcutta in 1966 for her mother's funeral, she answered an appeal from one of her teachers and Phyllis' famous coffee mornings were born. Between 1966-1992, she raised £12,500 for Mother Teresa and the Loreto Orphanage in Calcutta.

Sheila Monaghan was the Parish Treasurer and sat on the Finance Committee for many years. She was also very active in the SVP.

Molly Neame was very active in Parish social work and was a very successful fund-raiser for St.Augustine's. She ran the very successful Christmas Bazaar each year in the Assembly Hall. Received the Benemerenti Medal in 1975.

Tessa Negri. Taught at the Bennett Memorial School in Tunbridge Wells. In retirement, she was the Assistant Manager of the Soup Bowl for many years until it was closed in 2012. She is currently the Parish's Welfare Officer.

Allen (b.1919) & Josie Pease. Deputy Head of the Ridgeway School and organisers of the Sherwood Mass Centre after Rev. Noel Lewenz. President of the Tunbridge Wells Multiple Sclerosis Society for many years. A brilliant calligrapher. Made a Knight of the Order of the Holy Sepulchre in 2000.

Nick Pointer, choirmaster of the highly popular and much acclaimed Folk Choir since 1992.

Yvonne Pursey. Manager of the Soup Bowl for twenty years. In 1996, she was nominated 'Woman of the Year' by the Tunbridge Wells Soroptimist Club.

Hugh Reynolds (1902-1987) was a schoolmaster, but for relaxation was an actor. Born in 1902, he read Modern Languages at Oxford and came to Tunbridge Wells in 1925 to be a teacher at The Skinners' School, from which he retired as a senior master and Housemaster in 1967. He also became a Catholic in 1925. He never married and was very active in School, Town and Church activities. He always rode a bicycle and from 1922, he travelled widely in Europe every year except for the War years. For 40 years, he played in TWODS, the Tunbridge Wells Drama Club and the Tonbridge Theatre and Arts Club and sang in the Choral Society. He liked Dancing, both Ballet and Ballroom. He became a member of the Guild of the Blessed Sacrament when it was re-founded by Fr. Boniface in 1925 and remained a member all his life. He was also Chairman of the Newman Association (Circle) in Tunbridge Wells.

Christopher and Jo Storr. Now retired, he was Director of Education for the Archdiocese of Southwark. Parish Organist, and Traditional Choirmaster, since 1977. Both he and his wife were converts. She became Clerk to the Governors of St Gregory's School in 1985, was the Chair of the Governors from 1990-2000, retiring as a Governor in 2012. He was made a Knight of St. Gregory (KSG) in 2001.

John & Pauline Teague. In 1972, he was the first Head of the St.Margaret Clitherow Primary School in Tonbridge. He has held many positions in the Parish. In 1991 he was the first Parish Welfare Officer. He was the Parish Property Officer, managing six properties with up to 22 tenants. Organiser in the Parish of pilgrimages, holidays for the over 60s and day excursions. Very active in the SVP. In the Queen's Jubilee Honours of 2012, he was awarded the BEM for his work in the community.

Angela Treen, d. 2003. A gifted Welfare Officer reaching out to many people in the Parish and wider community. A key member of the parish social events committee. Founder of the Brownie Pack in St.Augustine's and District Commissioner for the Guides.

Tom & Laurentia Tully. Married in 1953. He a soft-spoken Scot, she from Belfast. 20 years with Daily Mirror Group which developed into IPC. Came to TW in 1962 for 7 years before going north in 1969 to Manchester to be the Sales Director for the IPC Magazine Division. They were a driving force in the establishment of Pembury as a Mass Centre in 1965. Directed the publicity for the GOD CAN campaign in 1968. Parish

Committee for new Church. They retired back to Tunbridge Wells, taking up their involvement almost where they had left off. She died in 2012.

William Vinehill was a staunch Catholic who had been the Verger for 42 years and sadly disapproved of Fr. Boniface. This led in 1934 to a confrontation between them, more details of which can be found on page 35.

Miss Elizabeth Wall (1886-1979) (known to everybody as Lottie) **& her younger brother Bernard Wall (1894-1976)**.

Lottie was to be St. Augustine's organist for over 30 years (1903-1933) and also its choirmistress for many. She had been discovered at Tonbridge at the age of eight by Canon Searle. His successor, Fr. Stapley, persuaded her to play the organ at St. Augustine's, first of all for the children's Benediction on Thursday afternoon, and then gradually moving up to High Mass on Sunday, accompanying the semi-professional singers of the Choir. In due course, she would be paid £20 a year as the Church organist. She became LRAM and taught music at Yardley Court, Tonbridge and Mayfield. She had a staunch ally in Fr. Trapp, who used to sing with the D'Oyly Carte Company and who was a curate from 1917 until his death in 1922; but she clashed with another curate, Fr. Desmond Coffey (1929-33), who was a great Plain Chant expert, and who set up what was a rival Plain Chant choir in the Parish. Lottie lost out in the clash and retired as organist and choirmistress.

Bernard Wall (1894-1978) served Mass at St. Augustine's at the age of six, went to the seminary at Wonersh at 18, was ordained at 26, returned much later to Wonersh as its Rector and in 1956 he succeeded Archbishop Beck as Bishop of Brentwood, for 13 years.

CATHOLIC MAYORS

There have been four Catholic Mayors of Tunbridge Wells since its incorporation in 1889. All have been since 1970, two as the Mayor of the Borough of *Royal* Tunbridge Wells and two as the Mayor of the Borough of Tunbridge Wells, the new local authority created in 1974:

Ronnie (Roland George Guy) Woodland, Mayor 1970-1. He and his wife, Mary, were Northerners, who came to Tunbridge Wells in 1947, and set up a fish restaurant. They were Anglo-Catholics and parishioners of St. Barnabas' in Tunbridge Wells, and they became Catholics in 1962. He was the Town's first Catholic Mayor and was made an Alderman.

Gerard (James Richard) Slater LLB, Mayor 1972-3. Another Northerner and a solicitor, who came to Tunbridge Wells in 1962 and settled in Rusthall. He gave his professional knowledge and skills freely to the Parish for many years, particularly over the building of the new church. He was the Town's first commuter Mayor with an office in London and Tunbridge Wells. He was the penultimate Mayor of the old Royal Borough of Tunbridge Wells.

Jimmy (James Bernard) Ludden KSG, Mayor 1983-4. Another Northerner. Headteacher of St. Augustine's School from 1954 and then the Headmaster of the new St. Gregory's School from 1965 until his retirement in 1983, when he became Mayor.

Alfred Joseph Baker BSc.(Soc), Dip.Ed., BA. Mayor 1998-9. Born in Tottenham, went to a Catholic school in Edmonton, left school at 14, and became a local government clerical officer. Then he took a degree and trained to be a teacher, and went to teach in Malawi. Returning to England, he became Head of the English Department at Sandown Court School in Tunbridge Wells. Has been both a Borough Councillor and a County Councillor.

CHURCH HONOURS

A number of parishioners have been honoured for their work for the Church by being awarded Papal Honours. Among these have been (it is impossible for this list to be definitive):

Knight of St. Gregory[13]

James Ludden,KSG 1983
Chris Storr, KSG 2001

Knight of the Order of the Holy Sepulchre[14]

Allen Pease,KHS, 2000

Benemerenti Medal[15]

Alfred Hubble (1885-1969) 1955
Reg & Bridget Argent, 1975
Neville & Edith Cox 1975
Leo (1900-1986) and Betty Kelly, 1975
Molly Neame, 1975

Note: The listings of individuals in this Chapter are *by no means* definitive and there will be many who deserve mention, who may have been unwittingly left out, *for which apologies are offered and hopefully accepted.*

---

[13] The **Papal Order of Saint Gregory** was founded by Pope Gregory XVI in 1831, in four classes. Awards of the Order are usually made on the recommendation of Diocesan Bishops for specific services. Unlike membership of the Military Orders (Malta, the Holy Sepulchre), membership of the Order does not impose any special obligations. It is thus the preferred award to acknowledge an individual's particular meritorious service to the Church.

[14] The **Equestrian Order of the Holy Sepulchre of Jerusalem** is a Catholic order of knighthood which traces its roots to the Crusades and to Godfrey of Bouillon, one of the principal leaders of the First Crusade. The Order is now primarily charitable and its awards honorific.

[15] The **Benemerenti (or Bene Merenti) medal** was first awarded by Pope Pius VI (1775–1799) as a military medal, but today it is essentially a civil award given as a mark of recognition for service to the Church.

CHAPTER 8   THE LIFE OF THE PARISH

The life of any Parish always has worship as its basis, from which all its other more diverse activities stem. St. Augustine's is no different and the different facets of its Parish life, together with the external factors and events which affected it, are reported below.

Church Services. The celebration of Mass is the most fundamental service of Catholicism and the number of Masses which can be celebrated obviously depends on the number of priests available. In the early days up till 1893 when there was only one priest, he was only able to say seven Masses a week. In the mid-19th century, there were only two services every Sunday: Mass in the morning, and Benediction in the afternoon/evening. Permission to celebrate more than one Mass a day however did come fairly early when more than one location had to be serviced. But it was a question of juggling priests and places and when in the 1960s, St. Augustine's had as many as six Mass Centres to service (with one Mass per Centre), as well as 4-5 Masses in the main Church (typically 5.45pm on Saturday and 8am, 9.30am, 11.15am and 5.45pm on Sunday) and there were only 4-5 priests in the Parish, it will be appreciated that even with a car (or cars), it was all rather a rush. Today we have three priests, but we still have five masses in the Church at the weekend.

Societies and Clubs. The extension of Parish worship into what might be termed 'extra-mural activities', namely Parish Societies and Clubs, depended on the social *mores* of the time and the needs of the Parish. It was certainly true that in the beginning of the Parish and probably up to the 20th century, there was a distinct class-polarity in the Parish, which was probably a deterrent to the formation of societies and clubs of a more social nature in the Parish, and those few that were formed were essentially worship-oriented. In the early days priests were more autocratic – they had to be – and the formation of Parish Societies was at that time very much at their behest, or at least with their approval. This situation was not something peculiar to St. Augustine's, but was rather a reflection of the habits and attitudes of the time which affected society at every level.

At the end of the 19th century, St. Augustine's had a choir, not all of whom were Catholic and some of whom were paid for their services, at a cost to the Parish of £100 a year. Their service also included giving occasional secular 'popular' concerts. There was also the Guild of St. Augustine chaired by Canon Searle, which met every Thursday from 8-10pm to hear lectures, have discussions and even listen to or watch entertainments. It was open to both men and women, but the names of its Vice-Presidents – the Marquess of Ashburnham, the Marquis de Misa, Lord William Nevill and Mr. William Bishop – does suggest that it was not particularly democratic and that the more humble members of the Parish probably did not participate.

In 1902 the Altar Society was formed with a strictly female membership. Its purpose was 'the adornment of the Sanctuary, vestments, candles, oil, altar cards, tabernacle veils and flowers' and this continued for many years, spending in 1906-7 £77-2s-6½d, which rose to £198-4s-1d in its 16th year, 1921-22.

But from the beginning of the 20th century, more societies began to form which were less worship-oriented. The Society of St. Vincent de Paul (SVP), caring for the poor and needy, existed from an early date and is still very active today, although there was a time when it went into hibernation. The Friends of the Sacred Heart and the Children of Mary were also very active during the war years. But it was probably with the arrival of Fr. Boniface, that the Parish had a priest who was enthusiastic about setting up Parish Societies and Clubs. 1924 saw the establishment of the Tunbridge Wells branch of the Catholic Women's League (CWL), which spawned in its turn the Union of Catholic Mothers (UCM) and the Girl Guides and in 1926 the Guild of the Blessed Sacrament was re-founded. From 1960-1985, there were also three sections of the evangelising Legion of Mary – for men, for women and for children – in the Parish, but it no longer exists in the Parish.

All organisations depend on the drive of their leadership and the enthusiasm of their members and if either falter, they slowly fade away or even stop abruptly, but then they can be resuscitated with new leadership and new blood. This was true, for example, of the CWL and the UCM which faded about 1930, but came alive again a few years later.

Organisations also change their names and their scope – for example, the Young Wives' Group of 1980 had become (possibly not surprisingly) the Young Wives' and Mothers' Group by 1990. They also change with the times – the Madonnas (a somewhat tongue-in-cheek name) were formed in 1999 to replace the Young Wives and Mothers. Others, having fulfilled a purpose, cease to exist. The Newman Society, the society for Catholic graduates, had a branch at St. Augustine's called the Newman Circle and was very active and avant-garde in the 1960s and early 1970s debating and discussing the future of the Church, but is no more because as one former member said 'We thought that there was no longer a need for it after Vatican II, but today we are not so sure'.

Interestingly, Societies and Clubs *as such* in the Parish are very much less prominent today. This may only be a change in what is currently socially-acceptable organisational nomenclature, with Societies and Clubs turning into Groups, but may also be due to changes in Catholic organisation since Vatican II and also in the priorities of the Parish. Since the early 1980s, it would seem that the organisations in the Parish have become less socially-orientated and more worship- and helping-orientated. This could be because the need for direct, immediate and local fund-raising, which lay under much of the Parish social activity and was so important in the 1950s-1980s, has become less pressing. It also reflects changing social circumstances. The Parish always used to have an Annual Parish Dance in the 1950s-1960s, usually held in the Assembly Hall or the Spa Hotel. This did have a fund-raising objective but it was also a congregation-bonding exercise. Times have changed.

Governance of the Parish and the Church. The biggest change in the governance of the Parish came in the late 1960s, when the first Parish Council was created in March 1969. This was a crucial period, not only in the history of our Parish which was taking on the Herculean task of funding and building a new church, but also in the history of the wider Church, absorbing and adjusting to the radical changes introduced by Vatican II, which brought about a change in the role of the laity and the scope of their involvement. The first Parish Council was chaired, very understandably and rightly, by the clergy. However Fr. Bill Howell, who was a shrewd, diplomatic and also a 'democratic' man, was proposing within three years, that it should have a lay chairperson. This was agreed and implemented and has remained so ever since. This does however create a potential conflict. By ancient Canon Law dating back centuries, which has not been changed significantly since Vatican II, the Parish Priest is still the ruler of his Parish and can have the last say in everything. The Parish Priest today has to walk a very diplomatic tightrope between the ancient and the modern.

The Parish Council has now evolved from the original Council, representing every aspect of the Parish through 6-8 Sub-Committees but appointed essentially by the Parish Priest, into one Parish Council with a Liturgy Committee and 37 'Groups' with varying degrees of impact, input, and frequency on Parish life:

- 6 'Uniform' Groups, such as the Scouts and Guides and their siblings;
- 8 Prayer Groups, with specific but different aims;
- 3 Choir Groups (Traditional, Folk and Taizé);
- 3 Charitable Groups (Outreach, SVP, and Kompong Thom in Cambodia);
- 4 Administrative Groups (Finance & Buildings, Church Cleaning, Flowers, and the 'Holy' Shop);
- 9 Support Groups (Baptism Preparation; Children's Liturgy; Catechists; First Holy Communion Preparation; Confirmation Preparation; RCIA/Journey of Faith (Rite of Christian Initiation for Adults/ Journey of Faith); Marriage Preparation; Bereavement; and ASDC [the Association of Separated and Divorced Catholics};
- 4 essentially-social Groups (Catenians; Madonnas; Over 60s [now the Tuesday Club]; and Prime Timers, who cater for the social needs of different groups).

Communication. Until the late 1950s, communication between priest and congregation was largely limited to sermons, notices from the pulpit (of which there are 20 volumes dating from the late 19th century in the Parish Archives), and face-to-face conversation after Mass, together with occasional leaflets and home-visits. That was all to change in 1960.

In February 1960, there appeared the first issue of **The Augustinian,** a monthly Octavo-size publication of (usually) 24-26 pages, printed on glossy paper and consisting of 11 pages of advertising, 10-12 pages of editorial, 2 pages of Parish notices and a cover. It cost 1/- (5p). The idea for it came from a Committee, chaired by Fr. Bill Howell, and it would continue as a publication until May 1974. It was a lively magazine with lots of news and photographs about the parish and parishioners, as well as general articles of a religious nature. It was a great success and much admired.

THE AUGUSTINIAN · 1/-

THE PARISH MAGAZINE OF ST. AUGUSTINE'S   TUNBRIDGE WELLS   JULY 6, 1969

It owed much of its success to its Editor, Ted Marchant, a parishioner, convert and journalist who brought his professional skills to bear from the first issue until he retired at the end of 1968. The magazine had been coming under the pressure of rising costs for some time and the change of Editor was a suitable point at which to change its format in January 1969 to a broadsheet newspaper format of 8 pages, still with glossy paper, advertising and a price of 1/-. This lasted until August 1970 when a further change, essentially to a slightly larger size and to a bi-monthly frequency, was made to try and save costs. But it proved insuperable and it ceased publication in May 1974. Additional factors in its demise must have been that the period from 1967-1975 was a very unsettling period for the parishioners of a Parish with no fixed abode; and with parishioners who shared the increasingly guilty and general awareness in the West of the poverty of the Third World.

It was succeeded in June 1974 by **St. Augustine's Bulletin**, at first a free 4-page roneo-ed A4 newsletter produced quarterly. This was very basic, but it probably fitted the mood of the times. It was essentially notices and information with little comment. Over time, the Bulletin became larger – 16 pages A5, stapled and with a cover from Easter 1981, increased to 36 pages by 1987. Its frequency then increased to monthly and publication continued to 1993. Since then, the printed means of communicating with the Parish has gone through a number of metamorphoses, seeking to balance reader-appeal against cost of production, but with the new and cheaper print technology now available, the Parish now receives a varied production – a 4-page full-colour A4 Newsletter once a month, supported by one 4-page black-and-white Newsletter and two 2-page BW Newsletters.

Musical Tradition of St. Augustine's. From the Archives it would seem that St. Augustine's has had quite a long history of 'musical excellence'. In the late 19th century, it had a paid choir which also gave non-religious performances. It has always had devoted organists and choir masters and mistresses and it and the Parish School have participated with some success in local Musical Festivals.

This was helped by Canon Keatinge buying a new organ for the Church in 1914 at a cost of £319 which was in use until 1967. Initially in 1975, the new Church in Crescent Road used a small electronic organ as a temporary measure until an organ made by Wood, Wordsworth & Co. was installed in 1980 at a cost of £10,000. In due course, this was deemed inadequate for the Church's needs and it was replaced in 1994 by a new organ made by Harrison & Harrison of Durham at a cost of £72,500. This organ is said to be the 'Rolls-Royce' of organs and on a par with organs in Westminster Abbey, St. Paul's and Westminster Cathedral.

The Wood Wordsworth organ was given to St. Gregory's School where it is still in use.

Of particular note in the Parish's musical history is the involvement of **Fr. George Trapp** [1917-1922], a former member of the D'Oyley Carte Company, who encouraged Lottie Wall in developing the Church Choir; and **Fr. Desmond Coffey** (1895-1977) **[1929-33]** who introduced a Plain Chant Choir to the Parish, which rivalled the established Church Choir and led to a 'showdown' with Lottie, in which she would almost inevitably lose out. Fr. Coffey also encouraged Miss Cosgrove of St. Augustine's School to enter her pupils in the Tunbridge Wells Musical Festival and they swept the board that year and for several years to come.

The Choir has since then had a number of devoted organists and choirmasters/ mistresses (the two roles seem almost inevitably to go together) who have continued the musical tradition. One development which reflects the change in the nature of music, both sacred and profane, in the past 50 years has been the development of the Parish having two Choirs – the Traditional and the Folk – which has caused a degree of friendly rivalry. They have recently been joined by a third Choir –the Taizé Choir – which performs at ecumenical services.

The First World War. All wars are traumatic and yet the perception of them by those involved can be very different. The First World War took a toll of Tunbridge Wells in terms of casualties which the Second did not. The names of 801 local men were put on the 1914-18 War Memorial at the Town Hall (including 25 who 'belonged' to St. Augustine's), while less than a quarter of that number (only 166) were added for the 1939-1945 War. However in other respects, the Second produced much more tension and stress.

The three biggest impacts of the First World War on St. Augustine's were the influx of Belgian refugees, who as Catholics naturally came to St. Augustine's for Mass; the treatment of many war-wounded at Tunbridge Wells' three hospitals, the largest of which, the General, was directly opposite the Church in Grosvenor Road; and the troops who were camped, billeted and bivouacked in and around Tunbridge Wells, while in transit or being trained before being sent to the Western Front.

The Belgian refugees were the first to arrive, as early as 18th October 1914, together with wounded Belgian and British soldiers. One entire Belgian village and its Mayor came to Tunbridge Wells as well as others from around Antwerp. They were given a sympathetic welcome by a friendly people and were accommodated, particularly in three large and empty mansions, but also with families all over the town. The Belgians were exemplary Catholics and their devotion caused Canon Keatinge to comment in a report to the Bishop that he wished "my own people (could) follow the excellent example of our Belgian guests and make more use of the ever open Church <u>on weekdays</u>". (His underlining. He did say however that the 10am Mass on Fridays, which had been designated by the Bishop as the 'Mass for Peace' [but was popularly known as the 'War Mass'] was very well attended.)

The Belgians were ministered to by their own priest, the Abbé Temmens, who lived in the Presbytery for the whole of the War, saying Mass for them on Sunday and preaching in Flemish and French. The death of the Mayor of the Belgian community and his Requiem impressed not only the congregation of St. Augustine's but the whole town as well. The whole Church was draped in black – Sanctuary, walls, carpets and even the statues – and the drapes were of such good quality and so voluminous, that they were used for black-out curtains in the Second World War.

A ward of wounded soldiers in the General Hospital, Grosvenor Road, c.1916

The war-wounded were a continuous presence and a continual reminder of the War. St. Augustine's clergy tended to them, along with their own chaplains, and the 'walking wounded' who were to be seen making their way around the Town and the Common in their distinctive blue hospital uniforms.

The third impact was troops staying in the area. This impacted in many different ways - there were romances and weddings, there were deaths, there was involvement in Parish activities and there was the additional need to provide pastoral care. The Army had its own system of Chaplains – indeed Canon Keatinge's younger brother, William, would become Chaplain-General (and a Bishop to boot) – but the presence of troops still involved the clergy of St. Augustine's which is best illustrated by two occurrences: the provision of two Masses, only for troops, at 9.15am and 10.15am on

Sundays; and the reading every Sunday of a list of those known to the Parish from whatever regiment which had stayed in Tunbridge Wells and known to have been killed. Some Sundays that list occupied more than a page of the weekly notices.

The Second World War. The experience of Tunbridge Wells in the Second World War was very different from its experience in the First. Then it was not in the Front Line. A solitary Zeppelin is reported to have flown over the town and dropped a bomb on the Calverley Grounds probably by accident, but nobody is quite sure where. Yes, it had quite a large number of refugees and there were a lot of wounded soldiers in its three hospitals and there were a large number of soldiers billeted around, but it was not the Front Line, which was somewhere in France a good 80-120 miles, and a whole English Channel, away.

In the Second World War, Tunbridge Wells was definitely in the Front Line. In August/September 1940, the Battle of Britain was fought in the skies above it and it was flown over on a daily basis by German bombers heading for London, Birmingham, Manchester and Liverpool. It was also a major area for marshalling troops and supplies in advance of the D-Day landings in 1944.

It is also difficult to appreciate today the fears that another war in 1939 only 20 years after the end of the previous one produced among everyone at that time. It was as near as events in 1993 are to us today. Fr. Boniface probably over-reacted on 3rd. September 1939 by immediately cancelling a 2s. (10p.) dance arranged for the Parish in the Florida Restaurant of the Ritz (later ABC) Cinema opposite the Town Hall on Wednesday 6th. September, as well as a Ladies' Retreat at the Sacred Heart Convent on the 10th and the Annual Pilgrimage to Canterbury on 17th , but the pressures and tensions were there.

On 31st August 1939, the Government had announced the immediate evacuation of 150,000 children from London and these started to arrive *the following day* – 1,400 at the West Station, 1,600 at High Brooms Station, 3,500 to Tonbridge, 1,000 to Paddock Wood, and 3,500 to rural areas. Virtually a whole Catholic School, St. Joseph's of Deptford, arrived on St. Augustine's door, to share the already overcrowded School premises in Hanover Road. The Infants' section of the School was immediately closed to make room for them, but it was not enough and the School started split sessions, with half the children attending in the morning and the other half in the afternoon. Fortunately the Deptford school had brought its teachers with it. The Deptford school was later evacuated to Devon when the bombing of London began.

There was much paranoia and panic at this time. All foreigners were regarded as 'Fifth Columnists' and on Sunday 11th May 1940, twenty 'aliens' were arrested in Tunbridge Wells, including two who were quietly removed from St. Augustine's without Canon Fennessey being aware of what had gone on, until after the service.

It must be said that Tunbridge Wells was not a serious candidate for deliberate German bombing, although it did receive a number of randomly-targeted V1s and V2s in 1944. During the War, it received only one serious air-raid on Thursday 12th September 1940 by a plane, flying from the west, which dropped at 5.05pm nine bombs which killed 15 people. In retrospect, this 'raid' was not planned or deliberate and was almost certainly a lone bomber flying back from attempting to bomb London, who decided to ditch his bomb payload on the nearest available town.

But one of those bombs (the seventh) fell in Grosvenor Road just outside the Presbytery door and the blast ripped off the stone façade of the Presbytery, creating the need for scaffolding until after the War and forcing the inhabitants of the Presbytery to live at the back of the house. It also broke many of the Church windows and damaged the clock in the Campanile. In all, it caused about £900 of damage at then current prices. In June 1942, Canon Fennessey received a cheque for £29-15s-0d war damage insurance to help pay for the damage. He also received in November 1940 a bill from J. C. Evershed, Watchmaker, Jeweller and silversmith, of 55 Grosvenor Road for £3-0s-0d for repairs to the Bell wires and Clock, arising from the bomb explosion.

The bomb could have had a more disastrous outcome. It was usual at 4pm on Thursday afternoons for the whole School to troop into the Church after school for Benediction. Fortunately the School was still on holiday, otherwise the result could have been deadly.

Service on the Lower Cricket Ground on the Common

The Year 1950 was both the Holy Year proclaimed by Pope Pius XII and the 100th Anniversary of the restoration of the Hierarchy in England. To celebrate this, the Parish – some five coachloads, say 150-200 parishioners – attended the Pageant and Solemn High Mass held in Wembley Stadium at the end of September before an audience of 85,000. The fare of 10/- (50p) a head to and from Wembley, included a three-course lunch. The Parish also held one of its regular Missions from 14th-28th May and one of the highlights of it was a public service held on the Lower Cricket Ground on the Common which was attended by well over 1,000.

The 'God Can' Campaign. At the end of March 1968, the Parish organised a week-long event in the Assembly Hall of Tunbridge Wells, at which every night well-known people, such as Andrew Cruickshank, Derek Nimmo, Lord Longford, Joan Turner and Monica Baldwin, spoke of their beliefs and the importance of God, to the accompaniment of Capt. Joy Webb and the Salvation Army Band. It proved to be a resounding success with over 1,000 people, many non-Catholic, at the Assembly Hall every night. So much so that the next issue of 'The Augustinian' reported it under the banner headline **'GOD DID...'** In retrospect and to give it a context, the campaign was not just to bring people back to God in what was an increasingly materialistic world, but also a very positive statement by St. Augustine's to the people of Tunbridge Wells, that while it no longer had a Church since it was actually in the process of demolition, it was still an active and vibrant community and was not going to disappear.

> **GOD CAN**
>
> **ASSEMBLY HALL**
> **TUNBRIDGE WELLS**
> **24th-31st MARCH-8p.m. NIGHTLY**
>
> **GOD CAN WEEK is sponsored by**
> **St. Augustines Catholic Church**
>
> *Appearing during God Can week:*
> ANDREW CRUIKSHANK (Dr. CAMERON)
> DEREK NIMMO
> JOAN TURNER
> Capt. JOY WEBB (Joy Strings)
> LORD LONGFORD
> PATRICK O'DONOVAN
> MONICA BALDWIN—Writer
>
> *You are assured of a warm welcome to these interesting and challenging evenings*
>
> Sunday 24th March
> Is God for Modern Man?
> Monday 25th March
> Can any Man help me?
> Tuesday 26th March
> Christ needs me
> Wednesday 27th March
> Worship—never on Sunday?
> Thursday 28th March
> Suffering?—Good God—No!
> Friday 29th March
> Forgiveness of Sin
> Saturday 30th March
> Death is NOT the end!
> Sunday 31st March
> United in Christ

Half-page advertisement in The Courier (then in a broadsheet format)

External Charity. Since about 1960, and particularly under the influence of the Second Vatican Council (Vatican II, 1962-1967), the whole Catholic world has become very conscious of the needs of the poor and deprived, and particularly those of the Third World. Consequently St. Augustine's has been very active in the past 50 years in giving to good causes and charities external to itself. This has taken a number of different forms – overseas projects such as Marumba in Africa and Kompong Thom in Cambodia; fund-raising for both overseas and UK needs through participation in Trade Craft and the Outreach Fund; and local funding and management of the Soup Bowl in Tunbridge Wells. A brief description of all these is given below.

Marumba. This was a project to build a dispensary/health centre at Marumba on the eastern shore of Lake Tanganyika for 30,000 Africans living in an area of 200 square miles. It arose in 1963 because Fr. William Burridge, a White Father (now known as Missionaries for Africa) came and preached very successfully. His sermon was short, he showed the congregation just one photograph and he raised £390 – roughly the price of a new car in those days. From there developed the project which opened a derelict shop at Fiveways for just three weeks and raised nearly £1,000 and from there, there was no looking back. The whole project was so successful that it was extended to build a second dispensary/health centre at another place called Muhinda. In all, St. Augustine's

The Muhinda Dispensary

collected £5,000 for both of them. All of this was to grow into the widespread practice in the Parish of Family Fasting on Fridays (not total fasting, but less food being eaten, with the money one would have spent on food being given to the CAFOD Fund) and into support for a number of CAFOD (Catholic Agency for Overseas Development) projects. One of these – the Catholic parish of Kompong Thom in Cambodia – would particularly catch the attention of Canon Michael Evans in the late 1990s and it became a major project for the Parish.

Kompong Thom is a commune (a number of clustered villages and hamlets) in the Province of Kamphong Thom in Central Cambodia. It is not far from Siem Reap, the site of Angkor Wat. Cambodia was devastated by the regime of Pol Pot, the Communist revolutionary who led the Khmer Rouge in the 1970s in a campaign of agrarian socialism, which caused the deaths in just five years of approximately 25 percent of the Cambodian population of 8 million, through the combined effect of mass executions, forced labour, malnutrition, and poor medical care.

CAFOD had identified the Parish as worthy of help and St. Augustine's rose to the challenge. Initially between 1997 and 2001, the Parish donated £31,000 to Cambodia through CAFOD and then in 2002 a separate Mittapeeap fund was set up for Kompong Thom which has raised £48,194 to date. There have also been separate Outreach collections which have raised a further £9,000, so in the past 16 years nearly £90,000 has been donated. The Parish formally 'twinned' itself to the Cambodian parish in 1997 and has had the Cambodian parish priest, Fr. Viney, on a 6-month stay in Tunbridge Wells to improve his English and gain experience of different parish work.

The Catholic Church at Kompong Thom,
built with the financial help of St. Augustine's Parish.

Trade Craft is a specific brand name, but it is also the generic name for the movement to give the primary producers of raw materials, particularly in the Third World, a fairer price and margin on the goods they produce and sell. Since the early 1960s, when this was first promoted by CAFOD, St. Augustine's has always supported it and their goods are on sale to parishioners after every Sunday Mass on 1-2 Sundays of every month.

St. Augustine's Outreach Fund was founded in July 1980 as a successor to the Brick Collection, the fund created in the 1960s to raise money to pay for the new Church, and whose purpose became redundant when the new Church had been paid for by 1979. At a public Parish meeting, it was agreed to continue with the fund-raising but to apply the money to good causes which were largely external to Parish activity, such as the support of Missionary activity, and a variety of home charities - the homeless, the handicapped, the blind, children, prisoners, the SVP, the Life movement and other charities, many local and most with no specific Catholic association or connection. There is a different beneficiary each week, candidate charities are chosen by a Committee of 12 and a collection is made after every Mass on Sunday. The Brick

Collections raised on average about £70 a week, the first Outreach Collection was £156, and then it rose to £495, a figure which it rarely drops below.

The Outreach Collection has always responded very generously to National and International Emergencies, as well as local, National and International charitable funds. The amount which is now raised each week varies and is currently between £400-£2,000, depending on the congregation's response to the particular cause. In 2011, the total amount raised by the Outreach Fund was £50,078.

Since the Outreach Collection started on 5th October 1980, nearly 33 years ago, the congregation of St. Augustine's Parish has donated over £2 million to the causes it has supported. It is an indication of a caring church that responds to the needs of others.

The Soup Bowl
The Soup Bowl was started in December 1991 in a small disused shop in Crescent Road owned by Tunbridge Wells Borough Council, almost opposite St. Augustine's, with the purpose of providing the homeless with nutrition, *but also company.* Since then, it has provided tea, coffee or soup, plus sandwiches, meals, biscuits and cakes to literally tens of thousands, averaging 50-100 'customers' a day. Regular customers seem to be men rather than women; particularly homeless young men aged 17-23; but there are older customers - 'travelling' men – some of whom have not eaten for 2-3 days on arrival.

The principal initiative for it, and its subsequent operation, has rested with St. Augustine's, in part because it was always the closest Church to the premises. But many of the other Churches in Tunbridge Wells also take an active part, mainly with financial support, and they should be recognised: All Saints, Langton Green; St. Barnabas; the Church of Christ; King Charles the Martyr; St. Mary's, Speldhurst; St. Peter's; and the United Reform Church. Other lay supporters, such as the Inner Wheel and the Land Registry, should also be recorded.

Over the years, it has provided a welcome refuge for many disadvantaged people - the poor and the homeless - who may not be the most socially-gifted of people, but deserve and need support. It is very sad that the Borough Council felt it necessary to withdraw their support and refuse a renewal of the lease in 2012, after over 20 years of operation, as a result of complaints made by new, *not the long-term*, neighbours of the Soup Bowl, about the behaviour of some of the disadvantaged 'customers' of the Soup Bowl.

The Parish 'Holy' Shop

The smallest Repository in the world? As it was in 1965.

Most churches have what is often called a 'repository' – a room or even only a glass-fronted cupboard stocking 'holy' items for sale, such as missals, rosaries, statues, crucifixes, religious books and pamphlets, and in the 21st century, audio and video tapes and discs of religious events, documentaries and music. St. Augustine's has had one for a long time. It was featured in The Augustinian in the 1960s as 'The Smallest Repository in the World?', but it is now very much bigger.

Since 1986 it has been revamped, due to the hard work of Margaret & John Elmslie and subsequently Ron & Jo Irons, Pam McCulloch, and Carrie Gates & Jennie Children, and is now housed in its own room which has in effect a shop window, just off the narthex of the Church. Its stock is much wider and includes cards for all occasions – Christmas, Easter, Mass intentions, sympathy, bereavement – as well as cribs and carvings.

Non-British parishioners

St. Augustine's has benefitted from having a number of non-British parishioners, starting with the French émigrés of 1848, the Italian refugees of 1860, the Belgian and French refugees of 1914 and 1940, most of whom returned home after the conflict. Two groups have however settled – the Poles of the 1940s and the 1990s, and the Filipinos of the 1990s and they are very welcome.

The exhibition which was mounted during the Parish Mission of 2011 showed that there were then over 40 nationalities within St. Augustine's congregation.

Poland

After World War II, many Polish people, who had served with the British Armed Forces, remained here fearing to return to a homeland under Communist rule. Some have been parishioners at St Augustine's ever since and the descendants of others are still parishioners.

In 1988, St. Augustine's decided to support St. Teresa's School for Blind and Partially-Sighted Children in Rabka in southern Poland with an annual collection of clothing, towels and toiletries. The School is run by a congregation of Franciscan sisters, the Servants of the Cross. By 2009, transport costs had risen so much that it made delivery uneconomic, so a monetary Outreach Collection was substituted and in 2010 the parish sent £1,000 for the replacement of windows at the school.

After the accession of the East European states to the European Union on 1st May 2004, the number of Polish parishioners greatly increased. Since 2006, the Polish Catholic Mission based in North London, has supplied a priest as chaplain of the Polish people in Kent. He comes to St Augustine's once a month, usually the 4th Sunday, to hear confessions and celebrate Mass in Polish. Some Slovak people also come to these services as he hears confessions in Slovak and Czech as well.

The Mass count for these special Sundays is variable, ranging from about 50 when people are away on holiday, to over 100. Mass counts for Christmas Eve and for Easter Sunday are higher - usually over 200 people - and over 300 people come for the East European Blessing of Easter Baskets on Holy Saturday morning.

The Philippines

In the 1990s, the demand by the NHS in the UK for trained medical (and particularly nursing) staff was such, that it conducted recruiting drives in other countries. An ideal target country for this was the Philippines, which had an essentially-American education system, had English as its *lingua franca,* but where salaries were low and therefore an English salary could be very attractive. This led to an influx of Filipinos into the UK and into Tunbridge Wells. The Philippines is of course a Catholic country and so St

Augustine's now has over 300 Filipino parishioners, who are mainly nurses and care assistants. Many of their children attend St. Augustine's School, and they are very involved in the life of the Church, as Welcomers, Ministers of Holy Communion and their children as Altar Servers.

St. Augustine's School

In the past 15-20 years, there has been considerable growth in immigration into Britain, particularly from Catholic countries such as Poland, the Czech Republic, India, Kerala and the Philippines. As a result, children whose parents were not born in Britain now account for approximately 20% of the School Roll.

English for Speakers of other Languages (ESOL)

In recent years, St. Augustine's has organised free lessons in 'English for Speakers of other Languages' for all its immigrant populations and as their English improves, it has enabled them to participate more fully in the English church services.

CHAPTER 9   THE SCHOOLS OF THE PARISH

The Schools of the Parish have developed from a single 'All Age' School for children aged 3-14 in the mid-19th century to a much larger Primary School for 5-11s and a very large Secondary Modern (now Comprehensive) School for 12-18s, both on separate sites, in the 21st century.

In between, as the structure and needs of Catholic education in Tunbridge Wells changed and developed, the original school of St. Augustine's grew in the middle of the 20th century with so many children of all ages, that it expanded into five different locations. However in the last third of the 20th century, this was rationalised into the two schools of today – St. Augustine's Primary School in Wilman Road and St. Gregory's Comprehensive School in nearby Reynolds Lane.

The first St. Augustine's School
The exact date of the foundation of the first school is uncertain, but there is an unverified statement from 1938 that it was built in 1852. It is clear however that it must have been well-established by 1867 when an announcement of Fr. Searle's appointment referred to the Mission as 'comprising so extensive a District, supporting the Poor Schools, and maintaining the fabrics of the Church, the Presbytery, and School'.

The first St. Augustine's School

The Planning Index of the Tunbridge Wells Borough Council records applications by the Rev. (sic) Searle relating to a Classroom in 1874, a School and Classrooms in 1878, and a School in 1879, and these must relate to the school building on the right-hand side of the Church in Hanover Road. There is a further application by the Trustees of St. Augustine's Church in 1887 for a 'Staircase to a Schoolroom' which must have been related to the Church crypt either being converted or 'modernised' into a Schoolroom at that time. In 1905 this crypt would be condemned for use as a Schoolroom by the Department of Education, which led to a further application in 1907, now by Canon Keatinge, for the new Schoolrooms which were built to replace the unsatisfactory crypt.

In 1899, when the Headteacher was Miss Mary Corrigan, the School had 101 pupils drawn mainly from the slums and tenements behind Calverley Road. Parents paid one penny per child per week (or two pennies, if they could afford it) so the School's direct income would have been less than £1 a week (there were then 240 pennies to the pound in those days) and the Government paid a grant of £38 a year towards the teachers' salaries.

It is also interesting to note that the School was given a whole day's holiday on 2nd May 1900, in order to join in the general euphoria which accompanied the Relief of Mafeking.[16]

It is not clear when the Committee of School Managers (now the Board of Governors) were first appointed, but there were generally six – half were Foundation Managers appointed by the Parish Priest, who was also usually the Chairman of the Committee; and half by the Borough Council and Local Education Authority (LEA). However the first extant Minutes of this Committee are dated 12th June 1903, with regular meetings stated to be held on the second Friday of each month at 6pm. This frequency continued for about ten years, but it is apparent with the coming of the First World War, that they became more spasmodic and after the War became quarterly and after about 1924, even less frequent. It is perhaps noteworthy that the Headteacher did not attend these Committee meetings until 1923.

---

[16] The Relief of Mafeking during the Boer War was the Victorian equivalent of Dunkirk in 1940 – a 'miraculous' escape from defeat (in this case, siege).

The first Minute Book of the School Managers in 1903 records the salaries of the three teachers. Miss Corrigan as Headteacher received £75 a year (as well as £40 pa in lieu of board and lodging) and her two assistants, Miss Woolcott and Miss Casey, received £70 and £65 respectively, which were quite reasonable salaries in those days. There were additionally two other 'helpers' – Edith Knight received 3/- (15p) a week as a ''Monitor' and 2/6d (12½p.) a week for cleaning the School; and Ellen Cribben received 2/6d and 2/- (10p.) for carrying out the same duties. So salaries and allowances came to about £280 a year, initially paid by the Parish but subsequently by the LEAs. If one adds in other running and maintenance costs (many of which were also paid by the LEA), it is clear that the School still needed a subsidy from the Parish to keep it going.

The succinct, unemotional reporting of the Minute Book also records the departure in September 1903 of Miss Corrigan, given three months' leave of absence on health grounds, but who seems to have retired a month later. Her replacement, a Miss M. Little lasted just one day, handing in her resignation the following morning, "declining to enter the school on account of the discipline of some of the scholars and saying she was returning to London at the earliest opportunity". The Minute Book records the sacking of Miss B. Hart and Edith Knight and Ellen Cribben, following a report by an HM Inspector.

The Minute Book also records the staffing of the School from 1902-23. This was in response to a request from the Local Education Authority for a reduction in staff numbers, presumably as an economy measure, a request which was categorically rejected. Staffing had been a consistent four over the 21 years, despite having been changed in 1918 from a Grade II to a Grade I School, which was largely a question of the numbers of pupils attending.

By 1920, the School had 130 children, four classes and four teachers all in three rooms – two senior classes shared the largest room and the juniors and infants were in the two smaller rooms. (See the blueprint on page 14 for the layout of the School in 1923.) The purchase of Brunswick Villa in Hanover Road by Canon Searle in 1889, using Benedetto Bianchi as the 'official' purchaser, did eventually allow some expansion of the School premises and playground through demolition of the house, but the School was never in very good condition and the purchase of Brunswick Villa was to be a financial liability to the Parish for many years.

The School in Hanover Road became increasingly overcrowded and this would lead eventually to it being spread across four–five sites in the 1950s before it was decided to split it into two schools – primary and secondary – on just two new sites.

By 1960, St. Augustine's School had grown to 370 pupils, 255 (129 boys, 106 girls) in the Primary section, 115 (66 boys, 49 girls) in the Secondary section, with a total of 4 non-Catholic children.

The Convent Schools of Tunbridge Wells

St. Augustine's Parish has also benefitted from the presence of two Convent Schools which came at the beginning of the 20th century, although neither still exist *as such.*[17]

Canon Searle, who in his early days had been Chaplain to the Convent of the Society of the Holy Child Jesus (SHCJ) at St. Leonard's for six years and had been instrumental in helping them to acquire the Old Palace at Mayfield as a Convent, spent much time trying to persuade them to open a Convent in Tunbridge Wells, but without success. (Among his motives for this, was that a convent would produce chaplaincy fees for the parish.)

The first Convent School in Tunbridge Wells was that of the **Sisters of the Blessed Sacrament**, then a mainly French order of nuns, who had been in England since 1874. They set up a Convent/School at 47, Upper Grosvenor Road in 1902 where 'lady boarders were received'. Canon Keatinge welcomed them and suggested an annual chaplaincy fee of £36, but when he realised how poor they were, he reduced the fee and gave them an immediate cheque for £5. The Convent developed and soon a larger house was needed and in 1912, the Sisters leased Misbourne House, 16 Calverley Park Gardens. The property was then bought by a friend of theirs, a Countess O'Cleary who paid £3,250 for it in

---

[17] The Parish has also had a third Convent – of the Sisters of the Holy Family – which was at 12 Cadogan Gardens, but this was not a School.

1915. The terms of their lease were improved considerably and the nuns had expectations that the house would eventually be theirs. However when the Countess died in 1919, they were shocked to discover that she had left it to the Sisters of Nazareth House in Hammersmith. Some swift negotiation took place and in April 1920, they offered the Sisters of Nazareth £1,000 and the property became theirs. The School was extended in 1923 and more classrooms were built in the 1930s.

The Sisters survived the War, although five bombs did actually fall in the garden of the Convent on 4th August 1940, but none of them exploded. By this time, probably because of the day school and in September 11 945 it had 117 boys and girls. By 1950, it had 147 pupils – 129 girls and 18 boys – and the fees were £4-10s-0d per term for day pupils and £7-10s-0d for boarders (of whom there were 12). In 1950, a new playground, with a netball and tennis court was added. There were 13 Sisters in the Community at this time, but the problem would develop of falling vocations (and therefore teacher-staffing problems) which would lead to the closure of the Convent in due course in 1962. At the time of closure, it had only 105 pupils, of whom 102 were girls and 67 non-Catholic. The Archdiocese bought the house from them in 1962 for £20,000 and the Parish modernised it and transferred the Infants from Hanover Road to it in 1963.

A second order of nuns – **the Society of the Sacred Heart** – opened a Convent School early in 1915, some 12 years after the Blessed Sacrament nuns. It was in a large house with 23 acres, called Beechwood, on Pembury Road. Their decision was based on several factors: Canon Keatinge, who like Canon Searle wanted nuns in Tunbridge Wells, had identified Beechwood as a suitable property and suggested it to the order, who inspected but rejected it in 1911. However the invasion of Belgium in 1914 meant that many members of the Order fled to England and so the proposal became feasible.

Beechwood Sacred Heart Convent & School

Additionally, Canon Keatinge had kept up a deluge of prayer about it for many years, and even surreptitiously buried holy medals in the grounds of Beechwood to encourage the outcome, so this may have had an effect as well.

Sacred Heart Beechwood exists to this day and will celebrate its centenary in 2015. It is however no longer run by nuns, who had insufficient members to run it, due to the general decline in vocations. They faced exactly the same problems as the Blessed Sacrament nuns, but they came to a different solution, partly based on somewhat different circumstances but also a different approach to the problem. Sacred Heart was a bigger school on a much bigger site and so had much more going for it to survive. But Sacred Heart also seems to have been willing to 'laicise' the school with lay teachers, which for whatever reason, Blessed Sacrament did not. Sacred Heart ceased to run the School in 1960, handing it over to an increasingly and finally total lay staff, although the Convent as such did not close until 1973.

In 1960, it had 234 pupils, of whom 232 were girls and 22 non-Catholic, a figure which has been improved on – in 1998, it was 266 - although there have been fluctuations. Since 1960, it has been a lay school, with a Nursery, Preparatory and Senior School for boys and girls aged 3-18, and with boarding facilities for girls aged 11-18. In this latter category, it has a number of overseas students, which has been a significant factor for all British boarding schools over the past 30-40 years. According to its website, "it retains its Catholic tradition and welcomes pupils of all faiths" and it is still regularly visited by the clergy of St. Augustine's.

The Reorganisation of Catholic Education Funding in the Diocese of Southwark.

In 1952, the Bishop of Southwark, Dr. Cyril Cowderoy, decided to reorganise and centralise the system of funding Church Schools in his Diocese. There had been a post-war surge in the birth rate, and there were not enough Catholic Schools, nor were they of adequate quality, to cope with it. There was also no sign of significant Government funding, so he decided to centralise all the individual School Funds into one Diocesan Development Fund; and to have parishes contribute to this by a levy which was calculated by the size of the parish.

At first, St Augustine's was assessed at £1,000 a year but for the next 20 years, it was regularly top of the list of parishes with a contribution of £4,000, raised by a series of bazaars and draws, including one in which the first prize was a Hillman Imp car. St. Augustine's had been quick to realise that by contributing more than requested, it could place them higher up the ladder when it came to fulfilment; and this proved to be the case.

The Development of St. Augustine's School
The overcrowding and the fragmentation of the school over several sites was clearly highly unsatisfactory and a determined effort was made to resolve the situation.

The 'architects' of this development were a team devoted to their cause: **Fr. Stephenson** the Parish Priest, his Senior curate **Fr. Nigel Larn**, **James Ludden** the Headteacher, **Fr. Bill Howell**, Fr. Stephenson's successor, and **Fr. Bernard Hegarty**, Fr. Larn's successor.

Fr. Stephenson has already been described in Chapter 4.

Fr. Larn, a convert while he read Greats at Oxford, was ordained in 1950, taught Classics for four years at the John Fisher School in Purley, before coming to St. Augustine's as a curate in 1954. He was the Bishop's personal representative on the Kent Education

Committee and was understandably well-informed. (In 1959, he moved to the Catholic Missionary Society and a year later became Director of the Catholic Enquiry Centre, before going to the Catholic Education Council. In 1965, he was appointed priest-in-charge of the newly created the new parish of Pembury and Paddock Wood.)

James Ludden, a Liverpudlian and familiarly known as 'Jimmy', became Headteacher of St. Augustine's in 1954 and in 1965 would become St. Gregory's first Headmaster, a post he held until his retirement in 1983.

Fr. Bill Howell has already been described in Chapter 4, and he would become the first Chairman of the Governors of St. Gregory's.

Fr. Bernard Hegarty served in North Africa during the Second World War, became an accountant and was a late vocation who was ordained in Rome in 1956. He was a curate at St. Augustine's from 1956-68. He succeeded Fr. Larn as the Bishop's representative on the KEC and was very well-respected by them. He played an important part in the establishment of the parish of Southborough, where he became Parish Priest from 1968-1975. (He moved subsequently to St. Thomas's at Canterbury, but continued working for the benefit of St. Gregory's and was made a Canon in 1974.)

Results from the team began to appear. Permission was given in 1955 to build a seven-room Primary/Junior School in Wilman Road, just south of the Tunbridge Wells /Southborough border, on land which until then was an orchard. In the early days, this school was sometimes called the Orchard School. The first classes were opened in May 1956 and 80 pupils moved from Hanover Road. The Ministry of Education paid £16,000 of the £46,000 cost, the Diocese the rest.

Four years later, in September 1960, the senior students (i.e. those aged 12-16) were moved from Hanover Road to the School's first Secondary Modern Department which was created in two three-storey mansions, 7 houses apart, in Broadwater Down – Nos.22 & 38. No. 22 was on loan from the Kent Education Committee and No. 38 was owned by the Parish. It cost £15,000 to adapt them, but there was no government grant for what was regarded as a conversion, and so the Diocese had to pick up the cost.

In 1961, three extra classrooms were added at Wilman Road, and their cost had to be met by the Diocese. With these and the move of the seniors to Broadwater Down, numbers at Hanover Road dwindled from 169 in 1959 to 46 in 1961. These 46 were the Infants' School and they would be moved in 1963 to 16, Calverley Park Gardens where the Blessed Sacrament Convent had closed in 1960 and which had been bought by the Parish.

The move of the Infants' School to No.16 had been intended to be a temporary one, but because of the economic climate, the Parish debt on the new Church and also some difficulties in getting County Council and Department of Education & Science approval, they were to stay there almost 20 years. In moving to the corner of Calverley Park Gardens and Pembury Road, the Infant's School acquired its own Headteacher, Mrs. Elizabeth Weir until December 1977 and Mrs. Mary Stacey until July 1982.

It was only when it became clear that the debt on the new Church had been paid off that a move of the Infants' School to Wilman Road could finally be considered. Then there arose a debate in the Parish about whether it should fund "a major caring project"[18] such as a home for the homeless, with the money it no longer had to provide for the Church debt, but it was decided that the next priority was Catholic Education and it was agreed that the Infants' School should merge with the Junior School in Wilman Road.

In 1963 the School building, built between 1877 and 1907, was finally empty after more than 80 years. This led to a renewal of the debate about the future of the Church building itself, the whole Hanover Road site and the structure and organisation of what was still known as St. Augustine's School, but which was in effect three separate schools, Infant, Primary and Secondary.

---

[18] The idea of a 'Caring Project' continued to be pursued and a house in Claremont Road was bought with a view to it being a home for homeless men.

What was theoretically one single all-age primary school taking pupils from 5-15 or 16, was spread over five widely-separated locations, which made it difficult to manage and coordinate.

The birth of St. Gregory's Catholic Comprehensive School.
Ignoring for the moment that the Infants' School was now in a separate place from the Juniors (but the intention was that they should merge again), the solution devised was to split St. Augustine's School in two, with a Primary School still called St. Augustine's on just one site for children up to the age of 11; and a totally new Secondary Modern School for pupils aged 12-18 on another totally different site. Since Pope Gregory had sent St. Augustine to convert the Angles/Angels/English, it seemed appropriate that St. Augustine's should call the new School St. Gregory's.

In hindsight, such a solution seems very clear, logical and straightforward, but at the time it was not so obvious and all the people involved had to work their way to it. There were many meetings and discussions, with Fr. Larn, Fr. Hegarty and Mr. Ludden playing major roles.

Following much lobbying and discussion, Kent Education Committee announced in April 1963 that a new Catholic Secondary Modern school with a capacity for 300 pupils would be built in Reynolds Lane, just within the Borough boundary and just south of Southborough, on what was open space which had been set aside for sports fields. It was also just across the London Road from St. Augustine's, 'the Orchard School', in Wilman Road, which would now develop further its primary education resources on this site.

St. Gregory's began as a single-storey building with a hall-cum-chapel, a Science laboratory, a Geography room and a Department for wood and metalwork. Its pupils came from all around – St. Augustine's Parish obviously, but also Southborough, Tonbridge, Sevenoaks, Paddock Wood, Goudhurst, and Edenbridge and East Sussex.

Building started in April 1964 and took a year. It was originally estimated to cost £100,000, but the final cost was £175,000, of which the Government paid its standard quota of 15%. The rest had to come from the Diocese and the parish and additional funding came from raffles, dances, whist drives and a profitable football pool, which was run by Fr. Hegarty and Mr. Ludden.

There was also the matter of appointing a Headteacher for this new school. Jimmy Ludden was the obvious candidate, but the rules said that there had to be competitive interviews. Six candidates were interviewed, and Jimmy Ludden was chosen and would remain Headteacher until his retirement in 1983.

St. Gregory's continued to expand under his direction, and with some assistance from Fr. Hegarty who continued to be involved although now in Canterbury. In 1978, it became the first Catholic Comprehensive School in Kent. It was very important that St. Gregory's should achieve Comprehensive status so that it could sit more equally with all the other existing selective schools in the area. The enhanced status and increased finance allowed Faculties to be created and attracted well-qualified staff. It is now a Mixed Comprehensive with currently 1,058 pupils.

To cope with the expansion, a second and a third storey was added to the School buildings. In 2004, a Sixth Form Centre was added at a cost of £1½ million and the School became a Specialist School in Mathematics and ICT and St. Augustine's Parish contributed £50,000 towards the cost. The Centre was opened in September 2004 by Fr. (now Bishop) Michael who had been an inspiration behind it, assisted by two other Bishops, Kieran Conry and John Hine.

Brian Keaveny succeeded Jimmy Ludden as Headteacher until 1994 and was followed by **Rosemary Olivier** until 2009. **Stephen Adamson** succeeded her as Headteacher.

Each Headteacher of St. Gregory's has made their own special contribution to the school: Jimmy Ludden in helping create it and being its first Headteacher; Brian Keaveny in developing a secondary modern school into a flourishing comprehensive school; Rosemary Olivier in raising the students' attainment, particularly in the Sixth Form, providing an education as good as that on offer in the town's grammar schools; and Stephen Adamson by continuing to keep St. Gregory's very much alive, both spiritually and academically.

St. Gregory's Catholic School

Headteachers of St. Augustine's School

No record exists of the staff before **Miss Corrigan**, who retired in 1903 through ill-health. Her immediate successor lasted one day before resigning, seemingly having been 'mistreated' by boy pupils on her first day.

Miss Mary MacFarlane, who had joined St. Augustine's in 1894, succeeded her and in March 1904 was appointed the first Head*mistress* of St. Augustine's school. After a number of unsatisfactory reports by HM School Inspectors who deemed her 'incompetent', she offered her resignation in March 1914, provided that she could retain her 'superannuation' i.e. her pension. Her offer seems to have been accepted. The HM Inspectors recommended that her replacement should be appointed from outside. The Board of Managers also decided that her replacement should be male 'in view of the rough nature of many of the boys.'

Frederick Sloman was appointed the first Head*master* in 1914, but died in October 1918, after only two days of illness, of the Spanish 'Flu. Because of the epidemic which swept Europe, the School was closed from 15th October to 8th November.

Miss Eileen Woolcott had come to St. Augustine's School in 1894 and was appointed Headteacher in November 1918 on the death of Mr. Sloman. She retired as Headteacher in 1932 and died early in 1933.

She was succeeded by **Miss Edith Gallagher**, who came to St. Augustine's in 1916, became Miss Woolcott's deputy in 1918 and headteacher in 1932 on Miss Woolcott's retirement. Miss Gallagher would retire at the end of 1950, when she was succeeded by Frank Walsh.

Miss Mary Cosgrave had attended the same College in Hull as Miss Gallagher, came to Tunbridge Wells in 1920 as Head of Music and trained the school choirs so well that they won all the prizes for their division in local musical festivals for a number of years. She would become deputy to Miss Gallagher in 1932 and would resign in 1944, dying in 1978.

Frank Walsh was the Headteacher from January 1951 to the end of 1953 and he was followed by **James Ludden** who was Headteacher until July 1965, when he was appointed the first Headmaster of the new St. Gregory's Secondary Modern (later Comprehensive) School.

Mr. Richard Meakins took over St. Augustine's from 'Jimmy' Ludden and remained Headteacher for 14 years until December 1979, when **Chris Foster** replaced him for the next 20 years until he retired because of ill-health in January 2001.

Mrs. Ellen Hoy was Acting Head from 1999 to 2001 and then Headteacher until she retired in 2006. **Mrs. Janet Mann,** who was the Deputy Head of St. Margaret Clitherow's Catholic Primary School in Tonbridge, succeeded her until 2012 and **Mrs. Jackie Warren** has been Headteacher since then.

CHAPTER 10. CHURCH FINANCES

Until fairly recently, St. Augustine's finances have been what could be called 'uncertain'. This was entirely usual for all churches, whether Catholic, Anglican or Non-Conformist, unless they were individually blessed with a patron or benefactor, since their income depended essentially on the size, wealth (or lack oit) and generosity of their congregation.

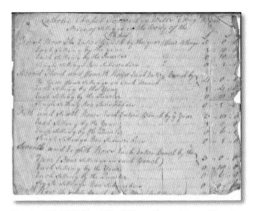

Part of 1838 Tariff of Bench or Pew Rents

Tunbridge Wells started out as a Jesuit 'mission' covering a much wider area than the parish does today. It was in effect subsidised by the Jesuits, who in choosing Tunbridge Wells as the centre of their 'mission' invested their own money, aided by public subscription, in building the original St. Augustine's in Hanover Road. Even they, while apparently accepting the capital cost of doing so, not unnaturally sought to raise enough money to cover the operating costs of running the church and they resorted to what was the (then) standard method used by the Anglican Church of bench or pew rents. There still exists in the Archives today a somewhat tattered, handwritten sheet of the charges made in 1838.

The rent for the whole of the front bench, which seated four, was £5 a year; the second, third and fourth pews were £4 each; the fifth and sixth £3-10-0; the seventh and eighth £3 and ninth and tenth £2. The Gallery was less expensive - £6 for the front row seating nine, with the five-seater back row costing £3. These charges were without doubt discriminatory - the rich were at the front, the poor were at the back, or even left standing, which they could do for free, but it was the common and accepted practice of the day and would not have aroused the disapproval which it does today. Bench or pew rents continued surprisingly at St. Augustine's until as late as the 1950s. Equally surprising is that there does not seem to be any specific record in the archives about the abolition, or the date of abolition, of what must have been seen by that time as elitist and very undemocratic.

It is clear that for at least the first 75 years, Church expenditure nearly always exceeded income. The bench/pew rent system introduced for very practical and necessary reasons, probably contributed to this situation, since it unwittingly discouraged additional donations or contributions, as it relieved most of the congregation from any feeling of, or responsibility for, having to contribute further.

There is no doubt that the cost of developing new parishes and buying property, such as Brunswick Villa in Hanover Road, contributed significantly to the deficit, but these were considered necessary expenditure if the Parish was to develop. In a Scrutiny Paper prepared for the 1894 Archdiocesan Synod, Canon Searle said that the Parish had never had any endowments, and that he himself had maintained it out of his own pocket as the congregation was small and poor. This would be repeated by Canon Keatinge in 1911 who wrote that he had been paying £200 a year out of his own private income to meet the deficit 'and I am now at the end of those resources. I have no debts but my purse is empty. My two predecessors died bankrupt; collections were made to pay their debts and clear their names. Such an ending I would fain avoid.' At that time, his annual expenditure was £695 while his receipts were about £400. By 31st July 1911, the deficit which he had underwritten had reached £1,195 in five years, despite making economies such as getting rid of the paid choir.

The situation did not improve. Canon Keatinge's return for 1917 showed that he had received £45-12s-0d from door money, £122-10s-0d in bench rents and £145 in Offertories – a total of £313-2s-0d – while his debts included £778-17s-0d still outstanding on the purchase of Brunswick Villa in 1888. However there always seems to have been someone or something which pulled the Parish back from the financial precipice.

In the 1920s and 1930s the Parish began to develop more of a social life which was a reflection of the easing of social class divisions after the First World War as well as a recognition of the needs to raise funds from all members of the Parish and social events were a means of doing this. Parish dances, weekly 'socials', whist drives and other social events developed rapidly under Fr. Boniface and were good not only for social integration in the Parish, but fund-raising as well. It would seem however that living on the edge of a financial precipice would continue until well after the Second World War when bench rents were abolished, proper Offertory collections were made, and the congregation learnt how to raise money by many other means as well, such as raffles, football pools and specific collections with very specific objectives, such as the Brick Collection.

Today, the Parish finances are in reasonably good shape. The famine of earlier years has gone, although it has not exactly become a feast. It is not the purpose of this history to provide a detailed analysis of the Parish's financial problems and how they were resolved, but certain general points can be made about the turnaround, which can be attributed to a number of inter-related factors:

- ❖ 1. The change post-1918 in the social attitude to supporting/ giving/donating, which was due to a combination of increasing incomes, more social awareness and a greater sense of personal responsibility and involvement.

- ❖ 2. Post-1918, the different approach to, and acceptance of, more social and 'commercial' fund-raising techniques, such as dances, socials, whist drives, raffles, tombolas and (eventually) football pools.

- ❖ 3. The final abolition of bench rents in the 1950s removed a number of inhibiting restraints, in both financial, sociological and psychological terms, on parishioners giving financial support to the parish.

- ❖ 4. The congregation of the Parish had increased considerably, particularly after the Second World War, which obviously led to more support and contributions.

- ❖ 5. An increase in legacies and bequests by parishioners, which are generally and largely unpredictable, but which increased considerably in the second half of the 20th century. Such payments are 'windfalls' but nonetheless very welcome.

❖ **6.** The need (particularly in the latter half of the 20th century) to buy property to achieve parochial aims (e.g. to provide a Mass Centre, school premises, or a home for the needy). However these aims/needs would sometimes prove in due course to be superfluous and be superceded. The property would then be redundant for its purpose. The sensible outcome was that it should now be disposed of. It would then be sold, which would result in a considerable profit because of property price inflation. In retrospect, this is probably the biggest single factor in the turnaround of the Parish's finances.

A general comment should be made about this analysis of the Parish's finances. The first 130-odd years are relatively simple – in general, the demands of expenditure exceeded those of income; and the Parish struggled to balance its books. The last 45 years are more complex because financial management and those managing it have become considerably more sophisticated. It is now much more complex to follow the financial trail, because properties are now owned, or bought, or sold, for very good financial reasons by different organisations – the Diocese or the Parish – and the financial or other involvement of other organisations, such as the Local Authority, the Local Education Authority or even Central Government, must also be taken into account. For this reason, this relatively short history does not seek to explore or draw conclusion about this Gordian Knot. However it should be put on record that Fr. Bill Howell and his Finance Committee and no doubt the Diocesan financial advisers (although they have a much lower profile in our archives), were the major influence in turning around the Parish's financial situation.

Let us look at the factors listed above in more detail:

There is little statistical evidence to support the contentions behind **Factors 1-3**, but common sense, together with an awareness of what life was like in those times, suggests that these factors are entirely plausible explanations.

Factor 4 is statistically indisputable and the supporting evidence will be found in Chapter 5 and Appendix 3.

Factor 5 is a relatively small but nonetheless significant input. Obviously, a single large legacy can skew contributions considerably (and they happen), but if one looks at them on the basis of a 20-year cycle, they even out, although obviously increasing with inflation. The total figures for each (broadly) 20 year period over the past 47 years, are as follows:

>   1943-1960 £   1,405
>   1961-1980 £   19,430
>   1981-2000 £   61,838

The vast majority of legacies are relatively small, but every period has had its major donors: Miss Ethel Burrows with £16,581 in 1979; George Dunkerley with £36,473 (including the sale of 10, Meadow Hill Road for £25,000) in 1981, A. Hemer (£5,000) in 1986, Capt. Norman Scallan (£5,000) in 1989, Mrs. H.A.Wellings (£4,213) in 1993 and Eugene Wan (£2,940) in 1989. There are also those who have left their houses to the Parish, such as Edith Cox in 1978 and Winifride Stonor who was particularly generous on more than one occasion. The value of both these two legacies are *additional* to the figures quoted above. The year 1982, which was also the year of the Papal Visit to Great Britain, was an exceptional year for receipts, with £113,000 coming from legacies and the sale of property. If there is any one year which could be said to be the turning point in the previous dismal history of the Parish finances, it is probably 1982.

Factor 6 is however the biggest single factor in the recent improvement in the Parish's finances. The properties acquired, and for what purpose, and disposed of, are listed below.

It should be made clear that the table below does not necessarily reflect a benefit to St. Augustine's Parish *as such*, since the *technical/legal* buyer/seller of a property may not be St. Augustine's Parish, but the Diocese; and consequently the beneficiary of such an action may be uncertain. In the end, this does not matter since the *ultimate* beneficiary is the Catholic Church.

Site/Property	Original Purpose	Purchase Price	Date	Disposal Price	Date
Hanover Road	Church	£756	1837	£80,000	1969
Brunswick Villa	School	£1,200	1888	Part of Hanover Rd. site	
The Hollies, Rusthall	Mass Centre	£4,000	1951	£325,000	2004
St. Joseph's Hall	Church	Part of The Hollies		£162,500	2003
Wilman Road	School	£?	1954		
38 Broadwater Down	School	£12,500	1960	£6,983	1968
16 Calverley Pk Gdns	School	£20,800	1962	£429,000	2002
The Annexe	Hostel	Part of 16 CPG		£90,000	1999
The Lodge	School	Part of 16 CPG		£30,000	1981
Reynolds Lane	School	£?	1963		
Hanover Hall	Church Hall	£38,000	1969	£100,000	2004
Greystones, Crescent Rd.	Church	£35,000	1969		
28 Claremont Road	Hostel	£?	1979	275,000	2000

The table above shows in retrospect a complex series of transactions over the past 175 years which were almost certainly not planned as such. They occurred relatively spontaneously, in response to a situation or a need which had arisen. They include:

* Purchase of land which was developed and is still owned (Wilman Rd., Reynolds Lane, Greystones)
* Purchase of land which was developed and has since been sold (Hanover Rd., Brunswick Villa)
* Purchase of property which was converted, extended or developed for a Parish purpose/use, but which has now been sold as redundant (The Hollies, St. Joseph's Church/Hall, Broadwater Down, Calverley Park Gardens, Hanover Hall, Claremont Road)

This is made more complex by the fact that some of these purchases and sales were by St. Augustine's, others by the Diocese. Most of the sales between 1998 and 2004 were made partly because of a change in Charity Commission regulations; and partly under the instruction of the Archbishop, since he felt that because of the change of use of buildings from the purpose for which they were first bought, the Parish had unwittingly developed into being a landlord and that it was inappropriate for the Parish to be in that role.

The cost of acquiring the land in Wilman Road and Reynolds Lane for St. Augustine's School and St. Gregory's School, together with the cost of building those Schools and extending them, has not been included in the above table, since they are never likely to be disposed of, in the foreseeable future. This is also true of Greystones (the site of St. Augustine's Church in Crescent Road), but the purchase price in 1969 has been included in the table to provide a comparison with that of Hanover Road in 1837.

The table above shows that between 1837-1979, St. Augustine's Church has paid at least £111,506 (plus the currently unknown cost of 28 Claremont Road) for properties bought; and between 1837-2004, had disposed of many of them with good reason for £1,499,000, which has obviously improved its balance sheet considerably. Nearly all of this disposal occurred between 1999-2004 which demonstrates the inexorable influence of price inflation. It should be said that there is nothing secret about these figures, since they are all in the public domain and available to anyone who chooses to search for them. It should also be recorded that while property price inflation was a major factor, the Parish had been putting itself gradually on a financial even keel, without it. In 1964, the Parish overdraft was approximately £43,000; by 1968, it was down to £21,000 and by 1979 to £4,000. Parish funds started to move into surplus in the late 1970's and the Parish started to lend money to the Diocese, which it has done so ever since. The property premium has therefore been a bonus, the icing on the cake.

While the overall capital account has improved considerably, it should also be recorded that this needs to be offset/counter-balanced by increased capital expenditure, such as the building costs for the Schools at Wilman Road and Reynolds Lane, St. Joseph's at Rusthall and more recently for both the Church and the Church Hall at Crescent Road, which have exceeded £1 million. Nonetheless, St. Augustine's balance sheet continues to look fairly healthy and it has been able to lend a significant amount to the Archdiocese to help poorer parishes.

It is not enough to look at Balance Sheets which record Current and Net Assets. They should also be compared with Income and Expenditure data which indicate the degree of financial pressure on those Assets. In terms of current operating costs, St. Augustine's Income and Expenditure broadly balance, with the former exceeding the latter most of the time. Income is now of the order of £200,000 a year. It employs about 12 people, nearly all on a part-time basis, with a salary bill of about £50,000 pa. Further costs include heating and lighting of about £12,000; telephone, postage and stationery of about £10,000; rates and insurance of about £9,000; and its dues to the Diocese and its supplies, repairs and maintenance each exceed £30,000. There is a risk that if the size of the congregation or its contribution to the Parish fell, then Expenditure would exceed Income and this could mean eating into the Capital Reserves with which it has been blessed in recent years.

What is true at present is that the Parish is in a position of relative financial stability, which is a far cry from the position it was in for its first 125 - 140 years.

Long may it continue.

THE FUTURE

Within the next 20 years, Christianity will be 2000 years old.

In that time, the teachings of Jesus Christ have remained unchanged, although their interpretation has varied over almost all those 2000 years.

The Catholic Church, descended directly from St. Peter, the first Apostle and the first Bishop of Rome, was the original Christian Church, at least in Europe. It has also had its fluctuations, as will any organisation, with changes of management and consequent changes in the calibre of that management.

Today the Catholic Church *as an organisation* may be far from perfect, but it has survived for nearly 2000 years because the teachings of Christ which are the bedrock of the Church, are eternal in their long-term relevance to everyone living in a world with six billion neighbours.

St. Augustine's future will be largely, *but not entirely*, dictated by what happens in the wider Church and World.

What we can say at present is that St. Augustine's seems to be in a fairly healthy state with a relatively stable (even growing) congregation, which is probably the largest Christian community in Tunbridge Wells.

However problems can be foreseen. The decline in vocations to the priesthood must mean fewer priests to guide us and provide the spiritual input and services which we need. This may require us to devise a different structure and organisation to cope with a changing situation. The increasing materialism of the world and its immediate and magnetic appeal to our selfish human nature, is also a major challenge to the less extrovert, but deeper, values which we should be maintaining and protecting.

St. Augustine's will undoubtedly change and adjust itself in the coming years, even if those changes are difficult to predict right now.

Only God and Time will tell.

1920

2013

ACKNOWLEDGEMENTS AND THANKS

Bridget Adam, Laurie & Marion Clegg, Rev. Kevin Dunne, Alf Hunt, Chris and Jo Storr and John Teague, for providing their knowledge of Parish events and people, and for their constructive advice and comments.
June Bridgman of Tunbridge Wells, for providing information on Protestant Tunbridge Wells in 1838.
Fr. Charles Briggs, Archivist of the Archdiocese of Southwark, for guiding the research.
Anna Edwards, Assistant Archivist, Jesuit Archives for guiding the research.
Ann Jenner for providing information on the Blessed Sacrament Convent.
Gillian Shinar, Bridget Adam, Pat Cookson and Carla Davis of St. Augustine's Parish for the long hours they spent trawling the Parish and other Archives and for their constructive advice and comments.

SOURCES

Archdiocese of Southwark Archives, Archbishop's House, 150 St. George's Rd, London SE16HX;
Jesuit Archives (Society of Jesus, British Province, Archives), 114 Mount St., London W1K 3AH:
St. Augustine's Church Archives, Tunbridge Wells

BIBLIOGRAPHY

Jane Bakowski: *Calm amid the Waves. A history of Beechwood Sacred Heart School, 1915-2004.* Beechwood Sacred Heart School, in association with Gresham Books Ltd, 2004.

Ted Marchant: *One Cog. A history of St. Augustine's Catholic Church in Tunbridge Wells 1838-1995.* Nd (but 1995 likely.)

Sr. M. Andrew Fulgoney, RSS; Sr. Christina Fitzgerald, RSS; & Sr. M. Zita Fogarty, RSS: *The Blessed Sacrament Sisters in England and Wales from 1874-1997* nd.

Royal Tunbridge Wells Civic Society: *400 Years of the Wells. A history of Tunbridge Wells.* ed. by John Cunningham, 2006; *The Residential Parks of Tunbridge Wells.* ed. by John Cunningham, 2004

APPENDIX 1   PRIESTS OF TUNBRIDGE WELLS

	7 Jesuit Missioners		Lived	At Tunbridge Wells, from/to	
Fr.	Randall	Lythgoe	d.1848	1838-40	
Fr.	Charles	Lomax		1839-40	
Fr.	James	Knight		1839-40	
Fr.	William	Rowe		1840-1	
Fr.	William	Waterton	1798-	1841-5	
Fr.	William	Rowe		1845-51	
Fr.	Thomas	Mann	1801-1877	1851-5	
Fr.	William	Rowe		1855-60	
Fr.	Thomas	Clark		1861-6	
10 Parish Priests and 5 Vicarii Adjutor					
Canon	Joseph	Searle	1825-1899	1867-99	died in post
Fr.	Charles	Stapley	d.1906	1899-06	died in post
Canon	James	Keatinge	1854-1923	1906-23	died in post
Fr.	Emmanuel	Morgan	1853-1929	1919	Vicarius Adj.
Fr.	.	Scholfield		1920	Vicarius Adj.
Fr.		Schmidt		1921	Vicarius Adj.
Fr.		Swanson OSB		1922	Vicarius Adj.
Fr.	Herbert	Evans	d.1923	1923	Vicarius Adj.
Fr.	George	Boniface	1874-1940	1923-40	died in post
Canon	Edward	Fennessey	1883-1953	1940-5	
Fr.	Arthur A	Dudley	1890-1949	1945-9	died in post
Canon	John	Stephenson	18 -1967	1949-67	died in post
Fr.	William	Howell	1925-2009	1967-95	
Canon	Michael	Evans	1951-2011	1995-2003	
Canon	Peter	Stodart	1947-	2003-	
65 Assistant Priests					
Fr.	John	Hayes	1870-1933	1894-6	
Fr.	Michael	Clark		1896-	
Fr.	James	Walsh	d.1929	1899-1904	PP Tonbridge

	Assistant Priests	Lived		At Tunbridge Wells, from/to	
Fr.	Charles	Keatinge	1857-1906	1906	
Fr.	Herbert	Calnan	1886-1959	1912-3	
Fr.	Edward	Mostyn	d.1936	1913-	
Fr.	Gerald	Sproston		1913-5	
Fr.	Thomas	Scott	1878-1974	1914-5	
Dr.	George	Hitchcock	1866-1922	1911	
Fr.	William	Curtin	1886-1930	1922	
Fr.	Bernard	Pearce	d.1947	1916-7	
Fr.	Charles	Trapp	d.1922	1917-22	died in post
Fr.	Hugh	Fickling	d.1936	1919-23	
Fr.	Joseph	O'Connor	d.1977	1923-33	
Fr.	Desmond	Coffey	1895-1977	1929-33	
Dr.	James	Bastible		1930-32	
Fr.	John	Rowan		1931-2	
Fr.	Daniel	O'Kane	1902-1944	1933-4	
Fr.	Lawrence	Oliver	d.1944	1934-6	
Fr.	Charles	Jones		1934-38	
Fr.	John	Byrne		1936-40	
Fr.	Patrick	O'Brien		1939-54	
Fr.	Herbert	Leech	1902-1941	1939-41	died in post
Fr.	John	Jones	-1949	1940-44	
Fr.	Barry	McGuire		1941-43	
Fr.	Albert(Dick)	Tomei	1906-1975	1941-44	
Fr.	Arthur	Woolmer		1943-50	
Fr.	Robert	Stuart		1944-47	
Fr.	Anthony	Cunningham	1917-	1947-8	
Fr.	John	Pledger	d.1983	1948-55	
Fr.	Peter	Freed		1951	
Fr.	Kenneth	McCarthy		1953-	
Fr.	Nigel	Larn	d.1998	1954-9	
Fr.	John	Bluett		1955	
Fr.	Bernard	Hegarty	d.1979	1956-68	
Fr.	Columban	Acton		1959-60	
Fr.	Mark	Quinn		1960	

	Assistant Priests		Lived	At Tunbridge Wells, from/to
Fr.	Dennis	Barry		
Fr.	Geoffrey	Nixon		1961-1971
Fr.	Michael	Bunce		1964-1971
Fr.	Hugh	Clarke	1920-1997	-
Fr.	Michael	Murphy		1968-9
Fr.	Paul	Weir		1968-72
Fr.	Hugh	Ryan	1908-90	1970-90
Fr.	Anthony	Porter		1971-6
Fr.	Denis	Paul		1971-
Fr.	Paddy	Cannon		1972-4
Fr.	Julian	Randall		1974-9
Fr.	Philip	Gilbert		1979-
Fr.	Douglas	Morris		1981-7
Fr.	Malcolm	McLennan		1986-
Fr.	Hugh	Bridge		1986-91
Fr.	Charles	Briggs		1987-92
Fr.	Martin	Edwards		1991-4
Fr.	Paul	Ryan		1992-4
Fr.	Geo'ben	Ezeani	from Nigeria	1994-97
Fr.	Matthew	Dickens		1994-2000
Fr.	Barry	Grant		1997-99
Fr.	Josaphat	Ezenwa	from Nigeria	2000-
Fr.	Liam	Gallagher		1999-2004
Fr.	John	Biju		
Fr.	Philip	Pak	South Korea	
Fr.	Marcus	Holden		2005-08
Fr.	Anthony	Cassidy,CSsR	1952-	2011-
	3 Deacons			
Rev.	Noel	Lewenz	d.1994	1981-1992
Rev.	Kevin	Dunne		1988-
Rev.	Donald	Coleman		1995-2003

APPENDIX 2   VISITING PRIESTS
(Most often in a 'Supply' capacity)

From	Date	Name
Wadhurst	1907-12	Frs. Hughes, Hart, Davies, Donnelly & Guise from 'The Mount', the Rosminian Novitiate, as weekend supply.
Holland	1952	Fr. Gerard Kruddei, returned for many years
		Fr. Weder, SJ
		Fr. Paul Klene, SJ
		Fr. Josef Scheiler-Amazaga, SJ
	1960	Fr. Jean Wester, SJ
	1966	Fr. Francois Meddens
Japan	1958	Fr. Peter Hameo (later Bishop of Tokyo)
	1960	Fr. Joseph Matsunaga (from Nagasaki)
Italy	1960	Fr. Mario Raguzzoni, SJ,
	1964	Fr. Filippo Casamassimo, returned in 1965
France		Abbé Jean Iramounho every summer for 20+ years
	1960	Abbé Helly
	1966	Abbé Jacques Dugas – a White Father
Thailand	1961	Fr. J.H.Thasundi Komkriss
	1963	Fr. Luke Banchong
China	1962	Fr. Aedan McGrath (Maynooth Society missionary)
	1968	Abbé Bernard Subervie (China missionary)
Argentina	1962	Fr. Enrique Moyano, SJ (from Buenos Aires)
Iraq	1963	Fr. Peter Haddad (Eastern Rite, studying in Rome)
Australia	1958	Fr. Leo Grant
	1961	Fr. Kevin Barry-Cotter (from New South Wales)
		Fr. Michael Keeting (from Western Australia)
		Fr. William Deery
	1964	Fr. Peter Kenny
		Fr. Bill Burston
	1965	Fr. Brian Byron
		Fr. Bernard Morellini (from WA)
	1966	Fr. Noel Grant, brother of Fr. Leo Grant
New Zealand	1964	Fr. Kevin Remy
Canada	1965	Fr. James Noonan
		Fr. William Hill
		Fr. Noel Cooper
		Fr. Bernard Woolcroft
U.S.A.	1966	Fr. Patrick O'Halloran, SJ
Peru	1966	Fr. José Davila
Kerala	1970	Fr. Kuruvilla Payngot (Malabar Rite)

APPENDIX 3
Comparative Parish Statistics

Year	1851	1925	1941	1945	1950	1960	1970	1980	1990	2000	2010
	No.	No.	No.	No.	No.	No.	No.	No.	No.	No.	No.
Est. Catholic population	na	750	na	1,800	2,000	4,800	4,000	4,000	4,500	4,500	7,380
Converts	na	9	5	13	11	26	4	8	5	14	6
Baptisms	na	32	39	104	81	95	72	66	72	57	75
First Communion	na	na	na	na	na	na	41	63	58	65	77
Confirmations*	na	0	0	0	106	13	176	63	60	41	26
Total Marriages	na	9	27	17	17	27	35	18	18	14	11
'Mixed' Marriages	na	7	15	13	11	18	24	14	14	10	4
Deaths**	na	na	na	na	15	29	26	36	30	46	38
Average Mass Attendance	100	462	838	863	950	1,833	1,641	1,278	1,281	1,241	1,018
No.of Masses on a Sunday***	1	3	4	8	8	10	11	6	5	5	5
Average Benediction Attendance	na	302	181	311	322	325	na	na	na	na	na

Until 1948, average Mass attendance was calculated on a count taken from 1st - 4th Sunday in Lent
From 1949, average Mass attendance was calculated on a count taken from 1st - 4th Sunday after Easter
In 1969, this was changed to the four weeks from 1st Sunday in May and in 1974 to the same in October.

na :not available
*Confirmations usually only held every 2-3 years.
** Data not collected until 1960
*** At main church, convents and Mass centres
Source : Annual Parish Returns: Diocesan Archives

APPENDIX 4   CURRENT PARISH BOUNDARIES

AS 'CANONICALLY ERECTED' IN 1970
(facsimile of original document)

BOUNDARY OF TUNBRIDGE WELLS PARISH

NORTH — From where the Civil Parish Boundary crosses the B.2176 east of Redleaf House, the boundary follows the Parish Boundary in a south easterly direction, across Penshurst Park and the River Medway to the Penshurst-Marlpit Corner Road. Then south east along this road to the point just north of the stream that runs southwards to Barden Mill Farm. From this point to the stream and along the stream past Barden Mill Farm, Blowers Hill and Mill Farm to Reynolds Lane. Then northwards along Reynolds Lane turning eastwards by the northern boundary of the Secondary Modern School to St. John's Road (A.26). South along St. John's Road to Powder Mill Lane and along Powder Mill Lane to where the Civil Parish boundary crosses the railway just south of Old Forge Farm. Thence east along this boundary to the A.21.

EAST — Thence in a southerly direction along the A.21 and A.263 to the Halls Hole Road. Then along the easternside of Halls Hole Road and the eastern side of the lane that leads to the footpath through High Wood. Then along this footpath to Reynard's Brook Farm on the County boundary.

SOUTH — Thence west along the Kent/Sussex County boundary to the River Medway.

WEST — North along the River Medway to Colliersland Bridge on B.2188 and from there north along B.2188 to where it goes over the River Eden. Then north along the River Eden to the lake north of Redleaf House. Then eastwards in a straight line north of Redleaf House and south of the Grove to point where the Civil Parish Boundary crosses the B.2176.

N.B. This boundary runs along the middle of all roads, rivers, streams and paths unless otherwise stated.

Date.. 17 Nov 1970 . :......   Signed................................

Boundary canonically erected on 24th November 1970

Archbishop of Southwark

Certified as a true copy of the original
J. McKettrick

Chancellor of Archdiocese.

INDEX

A
Adamson, Stephen   108
Altar Society   81
Amigo, Archbishop Peter   36, 39, 40, 42, 57(fn)
Annexe, The, 16 CPG   117
Annual Returns   51, Appendix 3
Apostolic Vicar   5
Argent, Reg & Bridget   70, 79
Arundel   9, 35, 41
Ashburnham, 5th Earl of   66, 81
Assistant Priests   31, 46, Appendix 1
Augustinian, The   43, 83-84, 96
Austro-Hungarian Empire 7

B
Baker, Alfred   78
Baptism   52, Appendix 3
Battle of Britain   88
Bayona, Count & Countess de   16, 18, 66
Beechwood Sacred Heart   27, 102-104
Belgian refugees   37, 86-87
Bench/pew rents   112,113
Benemerenti Medal   70, 72, 73, 75, 79
Bianchi, Benedetto   12, 34, 67, 100
Bishop, Mr. W.H.   67
Blessed Sacrament, Guild of   20, 36, 74
Blessed Sacrament, Sisters of 102-103, 106
Blueprint plan   14
Bombing of Tunbridge Wells 40, 88-89,106
Boniface, Fr. George   28-40
Bourne, Bishop (later Cardinal) Francis   68
Bowen, Archbishop Michael   28
Broadwater Down, No.38   106, 117
Brunswick Villa 12, 14, 34, 36, 100, 113, 117
Burrows, Miss Ethel   116
Burton, Decimus   4, 12

C
CAFOD   92-93
Calverley Grounds   24, 88
Calverley New Town   4, 12, 13
Calverley Park   26
Calverley Park Gardens, No.16   106 ,117
Card family, The   70
Catholic hierarchy, Restoration of   5
Catholic Relief Acts 2
Catholic Women's League (CWL) 72,   81-82
Census 4, 51
Chapel of King Charles the Martyr   3, 4, 94
Children, Jennie   95
Christchurch, High St.   4, 25

Choirs, Church   85-86
Church Services   80
Claremont Rd. No.28   26, 117-118
Clarke, Fr. Hugh   48
Clegg, Laurie & Marion   71
Cockerell, Eric   71
Coffey, Fr. Desmond   47, 77-78, 85-86
Coleman, Deacon Don   49
Communication   83-84
Confirmation   52, Appendix 3
Convent Schools   101-104
Converts to Catholicism 32, 34, 38, 40, 42, 52, 71, 74, 76
Corpus Christi procession   37
Corpus Christi Church, Tonbridge   8, 62
Corrigan, Miss Mary   100, 110
Cosgrave, Miss Mary   87, 110
Cowderoy, Archbishop Cyril 24, 28, 104
Cox, Edith   117
Cox, Neville & Edith   57, 79
Crescent Road   11, 20, 26, 27, 28, 49, 117
Cummings, Rev. John   13
Cundall's Garage   26

D
Darell family, the   3
Deaths (funerals)   53, Appendix 3
Dickens, Msgr. Matthew   48
Diocesan Development Fund   104
Diocesan Priests   32
Dudley, Fr. Arthur 32, 40-42, 57 (fn)
Dunkerley, George   117
Dunne, Deacon Kevin   49

E
Education Act of 1870   15
Elkingtons of Tonbridge   28, 60
Elmslie, John & Margaret   95
Elphick, Mr. Brett   18
Emmanuel Chapel/Church   4, 5, 27
English Reformation 1
ESOL courses   97
Evacuees   88
Evans, Canon (later Bishop) Michael 45
Evans, Fr. Herbert 32, 38

F
Fennessey, Canon Edward   40-41
Fenwick, Mrs. M.H.   15, 37, 59, 68-69
First Communions   52, Appendix 3
First World War   86-87, 102
Fooks, Edward   69
Foster, Chris   111
Fry, Elisabeth   5
Fuller, Lionel & Kathleen   72

G
Gallagher, Miss Edith   110
Gates, Carrie   95
Girl Guides   39, 81
'God Can' campaign 90-91
Gordon Riots in 1780   2
Government of Parish   82-83
Gower, Mr. (later Sir) Robert   20, 71
Gower, Pauline   71
Grant, Dr. Thomas, first Bishop of Southwark   33
Greystones   11, 26, 117
Griffiths, Bishop Thomas   31
Grosvenor Road   11, 12, 13, 15, 16, 18, 24, 44
Guild of Blessed Sacrament   20, 36, 74

H
Hanover Hall   119
Hanover Road   4, 11, 12, 13, 14, 18, 24, 34, 44, 49, 57, 105, 117
Harting family 3
Hawkenbury Cemetery   33, 39
Hegarty, Fr. Bernard   47, 60, 104-5, 108
Hemer, A.   117
Henry VIII   1
Hierarchy, Restoration of   5
Hoare, Canon Edward   5-6
Holy Family, Sisters of   101 (fn)
Holy Sepulchre, Order of   76, 79
Holy Trinity Church   4, 25
Hollies, The, Rusthall   62, 117
Hospitals, Tunbridge Wells   86, 87
Howell, Fr. William (Bill)   43-44, 104,115
Hoy, Mrs. Ellen   111
Hubble, Alfred 18, 19, 72, 79
Hughes, William Barnsley   59
Hunt, Alfred   72-73

I
Ireland, Joseph   13
Irish Potato Famine   3, 57
Irons, Ron & Jo   95

J

James I 1
Jarvis, John, builder 18
Jerningham family 3
Jesuits 6, 8, 12, 14, 31-33, Appendix 1
Jesuit Mission, boundaries of 6, 8-10

K

Keatinge, Bishop William 20, 36, 87
Keatinge, Canon 20, 35-37, 51, 85, 86, 87, 103, 113
Keatinge, Fr. Charles 36
Keaveny, Brian 108
Kelly, Leo & Betty 73, 79
Kelly, Fr. Peter 73
Kelly, Sr. Ann 73
Kompong Thom 45, 92-93

L

Larn, Fr. Nigel 47, 56, 94, 104-105
Legacies 116
Legion of Mary 81
Lewenz, Deacon Noel 49, 68
Long, Dr. William 24, 73
Long, Dr. Mary 24
Ludden, Jimmy 79, 104, 105, 108
Lythgoe, SJ, Fr. Randall 31

M

MacFarlane, Miss Mary 110
Mann, Mrs. Janet 111
Marchant, Ted 38, 74
Marriages 53, Appendix 3
Martin, Stanley 74
Marumba project 44, 91-92
Mass Centres 42, 46, 57; Chapter 6 passim
Mayfield 32, 38, 101
McCulloch, Malcolm & Pam 74, 95
McGuire, Mrs. Lilian 43, 74-75
Meakins, Mr. Richard 111
Milner, Phyllis 75
Misa, Marques & Marquesa de 59, 66
Monaghan, Sheila 75
Montpensier, Antoine, Duc de 65-66
Musical Tradition of Parish 85

N

Neame, Molly 75, 79
Negri, Tessa 75
Nevill, Lord William 66, 67
Newman, John Henry, Cardinal 5(fn)
Newman Society (Circle) 71, 82
No. of Sunday Masses 54-55, Appendix.3

O
Olivier, Rosemary   110
Ordinariate of Our Lady of Walsingham   61
Organs, Church   86
Outreach Fund, St. Augustine's   43, 93-94
Oxford Movement   5(fn)

P
Paddock Wood, St. Justus   8, 52, 55-56
Papal Bull *Universalis Ecclesiae*   6
Papal States   1(fn), 7
Parish balance sheet   118-119
Parish Council   82-83
Parish income & expenditure   118-119
Parish 'Holy' Shop   95
Parish statistics   Chapter 5, Appendix 3
Pease, Allen & Josie   75, 79
Pembury, St. Anselm's   8, 52, 55-56
Penshurst, St. Gregory's   58, 63
Pevsner Architectural Guide to Kent   28
Philippines, The, & Filipinos   96, 97
Pointer, Nick   76
Poland and the Polish   96
Population of Tunbridge Wells   4, 5
Property Sales   115,117 118
Pursey, Yvonne   76

Q
Quakers   5
Queen Maria Amalia of France   65
Queen Victoria   5, 14, 30

R
Ramslye   58,62
Redding, Fr. Frederic   60
Reich, Ludwig   70
Reynolds, Hugh   76
Reynolds Lane   11   107,117, 118
Ross, Dr. Ken & Dr. Mary   11, 26
Rustall, St. Joseph's   62, 63
Ryan, Fr. Hugh   48

S
Sacred Heart Convent & School   10, 33, 37, 102, 103
Salter, Fr. Reginald   54
Scallan, Capt. Norman   116
School Managers' Minute Book   100
Scotney Castle   3
Searle, Canon Joseph   13, 29-31, 46, 53, 60, 98, 100, 102
Second World War   88-89, 102
Sherwood   58
Size of Congregation   22, 39, 46, 47, App.3

Slater, Gerard   71
Sloman, Frederick   110
Smith, Archbishop Peter   45
Societies & Clubs, Parish   73
Soup Bowl, The   94-95
Southborough, St. Dunstan's 25, 58, 59-61
Special Branch   40
St. Augustine's:
   Campanile   15, 16-19, 89
   Church   p*assim*
   Church Hall   28,29
   Parish   *passim*
   Presbytery   13, 19, 33
   School   *passim* (esp. Chapter 9)
St. Barnabas's Church   5, 94
St. Dunstan's Church, Southborough   25, 58, 59-61
St. Gregory, Order of   79
St. Gregory's School   11, 25, 55, 107, 109
St. James's Church   5
St. John's Church   5
St. Joseph's Hall, Rusthall   62
St. Joseph's School Deptford   88-89
St. Peter's Church   5, 94
St. Stephen's Mission Chapel   5
St. Tesco's   11, 25-26
Stacey, Mrs. Mary   106
Stapley, Canon Charles 18, 34-35, 58
Stephenson, Canon John 32, 104
Stodart, Canon Peter 46
Stonor, Miss Winifride   116
Storr, Christopher & Jo 76, 79
SVP (Society of St. Vincent de Paul) 73, 75, 77, 81

T
Tankerville, Countess   26
Teague, John & Pauline 76-77
Tesco Supermarkets 11,25-27
Tomei, Fr. Albert   47
Tonbridge, Corpus Christi   9, 52, 58-59
Tradecraft   93
Trapp, Fr. Charles 38, 47, 86
Travelling Mission   41
Treen, Angela   77
Tully, Tom & Laurentia   77
Tunbridge Wells Borough Council 10, 22, 24, 26, 29, 94, 99
Tunbridge Wells Christian Fellowship   29

U
Union of Catholic Mothers (UCM) 39, 81-82

V
Vatican II 35, 44, 82, 83, 91
VI & V2 missiles 89
Vicarius Adjutor 31, 32, 37, 38, 42, 43
Vinehill, William 18, 39, 77

W
Wadhurst, Sacred Heart 9, 36
Wall, Fr. (later Bishop) Bernard 65, 70
Miss Elizabeth Wall, (Lottie) 35, 70
Walsh, Frank 111
Walsh, Fr. James 42
Wan, Eugene 116
War, First World 86-87
War, Second World 88-89
War wounded 86-87, 88
Ward, John 11
War Memorials 20-21, 86
Warren, Mrs. Jackie 111
Weir, Mrs. Elisabeth 106
Wellings, Mrs H. A. 116
Westminster Chimes/Quarters 16, 17
Whetenhall family 3
Whyborne family 3
Wilman Road 105-107, 117
Woodland, Ronnie 79
Woolcott, Miss Eileen 100, 111

Y
Year 1950 90
Young Wives' Group 82

Z
Zeppelin 88
Zollverein 7